Hours of Work

INDUSTRIAL RELATIONS RESEARCH ASSOCIATION

PUBLICATION NO. 32

(The previous books in this series were published by the Association in Madison, Wisconsin, with the exception of No. 11, Manpower in the United States, No. 15, Emergency Disputes and National Policy, No. 17, Research in Industrial Human Relations, No. 19, A Decade of Industrial Relations Research: 1946–1956, No. 21, New Dimensions in Collective Bargaining, No. 23, Employment Relations Research, No. 27, Public Policy and Collective Bargaining, No. 29, Adjusting to Technological Change, and No. 31, Regulating Union Government, which were published by Harper & Row, Publishers, New York.)

HOURS OF WORK

EDITED BY **Clyde E. Dankert**
Dartmouth College

Floyd C. Mann
Institute for Social Research
The University of Michigan

Herbert R. Northrup
Wharton School of Finance and Commerce
University of Pennsylvania

HARPER & ROW, PUBLISHERS, NEW YORK

FIRST EDITION

LIBRARY OF CONGRESS CATALOG CARD NUMBER: 65-21007

H-P

Contents

Preface

One of the most widely discussed issues in the field of industrial relations during the last decade has been the question of hours of work. Organized labor has been particularly interested in the problem, and many unions have pressed for a reduction not only in the length of the workweek but in the length of the workyear as well. Indeed, through their advocacy of earlier retirement for industrial workers, they have in addition sought a decrease in the length of the worklife. Employers too have been keenly interested in the hours question, and the matter has also attracted widespread attention among the members of the general public, including academicians. Economists, sociologists, and psychologists—to name but three groups—have probed increasingly into the problem and have contributed much to our understanding of it.

Some of the results of the work of academicians in this highly important area of study are set forth in the eleven chapters that follow. In a book of this sort, in contrast to one written by a single author, it is almost inevitable that there will be gaps in the general presentation of the subject, as well as a certain amount of repetition. An attempt has been made, however, to keep the repetition to a minimum, and it is the hope of the editors that the gaps will not be too serious.

The recent wave of interest in the hours question has been attributable largely to continuing unemployment. Since this problem has not been solved, the question of hours of work is still with us. The chapters in the present volume should furnish us not only with a certain amount of historical perspective on this continuing issue, but should acquaint us with some of its most significant contemporary aspects.

Clyde E. Dankert
Floyd C. Mann
Herbert R. Northrup

April 1965

Hours of Work

1. The Reduction in Hours

HERBERT R. NORTHRUP
Department of Industry
Wharton School of Finance and Commerce
University of Pennsylvania

For 1840, the average workweek was estimated at 69 hours in England, 78 in the United States and France, and 83 in Germany.[1] Based on life in this period, Karl Marx predicted an ever worsening of the wage earner's position—a position which in terms of hours and wages became, on the contrary, ever superior for the next 125 years. With hours, the subject of this chapter and book, we may well begin by asking what has led to the reduced hours which have accompanied the increased real wages over the years.

Competitive Tendency toward Shorter Hours

Most economists agree that a competitive economy, including our own imperfect one, tends to ensure a rising level of real wages because of the individual efforts of employers to secure a maximum return.[2] Can the same sanguine result be predicted with regard to shortening of the hours of work? Is there any long-run tendency in a capitalistic society toward shorter hours of work, or have the gains which have been scored in this direction been obtained largely

1

through governmental regulation and the concerted efforts of organized labor?

An important theoretical distinction suggests itself: The twin objectives of higher real wages and shorter hours are not attained by the same economic paths. A hypothetical example will make this clear. Assume an economic society in which the labor market is composed of individual pools of labor with zero mobility between the various pools. (This might be the case if industry were located exclusively in small towns which workers were loath to leave even if wage rates were considerably reduced.) Assume further that each pool of labor is dependent for employment on one employer who takes advantage of his position by paying wages below the marginal revenue productivity of his workers and by maintaining this low wage level despite rising labor productivity incidental to technological progress. Under even these highly unrealistic assumptions, heavily weighted against labor, real wages would nevertheless show a tendency to rise, since the level of real wages is determined not only by competition in the labor market but also by competition in the product market; and workers, even though deprived of the ability to obtain their full marginal-productivity wage, are not thereby deprived of the full bargaining power which they exercise in their roles as consumers and final arbiters of the competitive process.

But does this twofold mechanism operate to reduce hours of work as it does to increase real wages? Suppose that as technological progress reduces unit costs, the employers in our hypothetical economy refuse to reduce hours of work and continue to work their employees the same hours as before. It is obvious that this will result in a greatly augmented output, consequent falling prices, and rising real wages. But there would seem to be no economic necessity that hours be reduced, except possibly as workers voluntarily agree to share work to relieve the burden of technological unemployment.

The conditions of this example are, of course, highly artificial. In reality, labor is not so immobile and employers are not free to dictate work hours. Consequently, as capital accumulation increases the demand for labor, competitive bidding by large and small enterprises for the services of labor tends not only to raise their real wages but also, to some extent at least, to reduce the hours of work. The employer who makes the most attractive wage and hour offer will attract the best workers, and this motive has inspired many farseeing industrialists to champion the cause of the shorter workweek.

Nevertheless, examination of the history of the shorter-hour movement in the United States suggests that the purely *competitive* tendency toward shorter hours has evidenced itself with much less vigor than the tendency toward higher real wages. Indeed, in 1922, the steel industry—then the basic industry of the economy—had so far resisted any trend to shortening of hours that the 12-hour day continued to be customary practice in the mills, due, in part, to the large proportion of immigrants in the labor force. In 1919, the year that 300,000 steelworkers struck in vain for the elimination of the 12-hour day, average weekly hours were 68.7, and an estimated 52.4 per cent of United States Steel Corporation employees were on a 12-hour shift.[3] As late as May 1923, the American Iron and Steel Institute declared that elimination of the 12-hour day was not feasible, but adverse public opinion finally compelled the industry to reverse itself.

The Technological Basis for Shorter Hours

As a historical development, shortening of hours of work has involved a dual process. On the one hand, certain factors have made possible a shortening of working time without any impairment in the standard of living of the mass of workers. On the other hand, certain forces have been most active in translating this possibility into reality. It will be convenient to consider the history of the shorter-hour movement from these two points of view.

As far as the real basis for shorter hours is concerned, there can be little room for argument. Union organization alone certainly can claim no magic elixir by which it can create shorter hours for labor with undiminished *real* weekly earnings. Of course, through bargaining power, unions can obtain shorter hours of work with undiminished *money* earnings; but this will simply produce a general rise in unit labor costs and prices throughout the economy. The reduction in hours of work, unless compensated by increased labor effort, will diminish the total aggregate of real output. Consequently, even if labor's money earnings are maintained, the decline in production and rise in prices will reduce labor's real wage.

The statement is sometimes made that the increasing productivity *of labor* has made possible a shortening of hours of work over the years. Does this mean that employees by and large work harder or put forth more effort today than they did fifty years ago? Or are workers more productive today because the labor force on the average has a higher degree of skill? Neither of these possibilities affords the real explanation for the growth in labor productivity. Indeed, the term "labor productivity" is something of a misnomer. It is simply a statistic obtained by dividing output by man-hours worked. The fact that the resultant quotient is termed *"labor* productivity" should not be interpreted as implying that labor, rather than other factors, is responsible for any increase in the value of the figure. Rising labor productivity is largely a manifestation of the joint contribution of increasing capital, improved managerial technique, and scientific advance.

Shorter hours and higher pay in American industry have resulted from application of labor-saving machinery and improved production methods which have enabled the American worker to produce greater quantities of goods in less time than workers in any other country of the world. Capital per worker in manufacturing rose from about $557 per worker in 1850 to nearly $18,227 per worker in 1960.[4] At the same time, output per worker has been increasing between 2 and 3 per cent per year. Labor in the aggregate has become more productive because it has been used in roundabout, "capitalistic" processes to fashion tools and build machines rather than to concentrate on consumer goods and leave labor to work unaided by technology. Science and saving, both of which promote the wider use of the roundabout method of production, are the two partners which have set the technological basis for shorter hours in industry.

The Shorter-Hour Movement

The second aspect of the hours problem is subject to more controversy. Capital accumulation has made possible the shortening of hours, but would it have materialized had it not been for the agitation of organized labor and liberal groups, and the legislation of state and federal governments? In the following two chapters, the influences of unions and government are examined and the effects of agitation, pressure, and laws are evaluated. It will be found that the drop in the workweek since 1850 (see Figure 1) owes much to actions of unions and government. But although the data in Figure 1 demonstrate that, except during World War II, the trend of hours has been downward since the middle of the past century, the efforts of the unions and of their friends in and out of government have lowered the average workweek but very slightly since the end of hostilities in 1945. The Fair Labor Standards Act of 1938 contains the basic regulation of hours and its hours requirements—in contrast to those pertaining to minimum wages—have not been liberalized since enactment except by extending coverage to previously exempt groups.

The scheduled 40-hour week remained the average as well as the legal standard through 1964, but several significant groups do regularly work less. The largest group among these is the big city office workers, nearly all of whom are nonunion. They suffer the rigors of commuting, which extends their period away from home, but once they arrive at the office, they are usually detained only seven hours per day, five days per week. In Chapter 8, the hours experience of such employees is examined in detail.

Among unionized groups, scheduled hours of less than 40 are found most commonly in building construction, needle trades, printing trades, breweries, coal mining and longshoring. The rubber industry in Akron, Ohio, went on a six-day, 36-hour schedule in 1936,

FIGURE 1.   AVERAGE WEEKLY HOURS FROM 1850

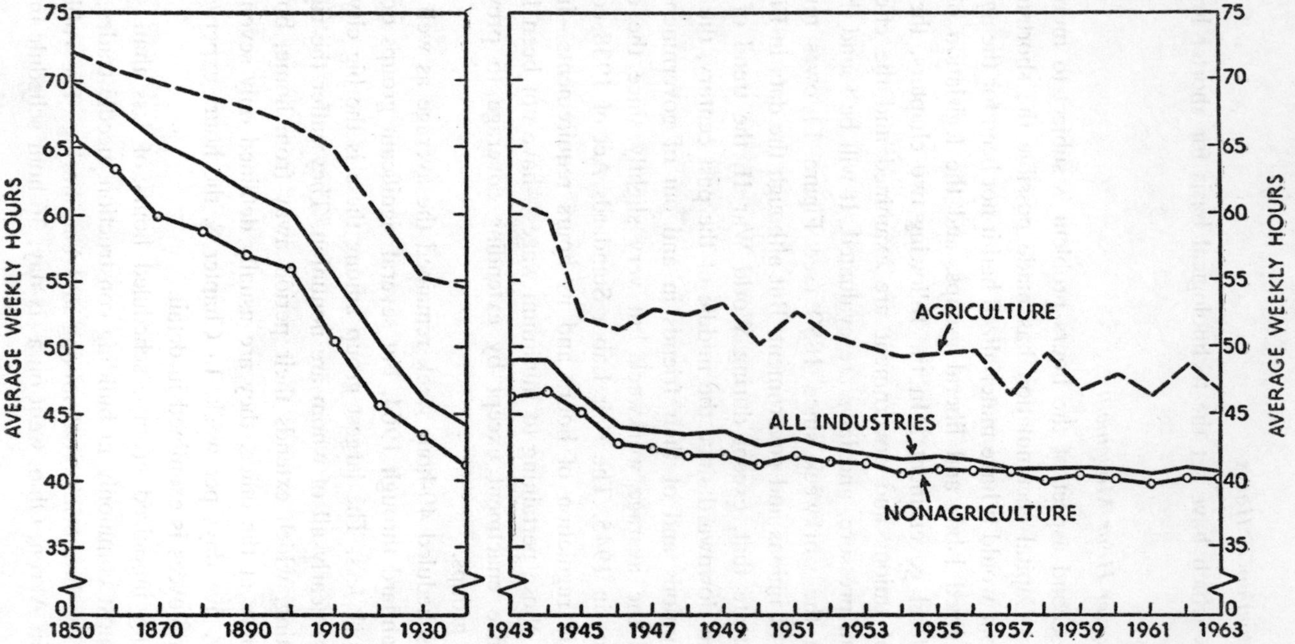

SOURCE: U.S. Bureau of Labor Statistics. Chart courtesy of Richard D Irwin, Inc.

and has continued it in that city, but not elsewhere. In general, however, 40 hours remains the factory standard.

Shorter Workyear

But if unions cannot be credited with much success in reducing the scheduled workweek below 40 hours, they have certainly scored in reducing the workyear by obtaining the benefits of paid leisure for their members. A majority of unionized employees (and many non-union ones as well) in nonagricultural jobs enjoy at least eight paid holidays per year. Two-week vacations are now general, with the seniority requirements for three- and four-week vacations being steadily lowered from 15 to 10 and 25 to 15 years' service, respectively. In 1963, the United Steelworkers negotiated the first "sabbaticals"—13 weeks off every five years for long service employees in the steel, can, and aluminum industries.[5] If the net effect of holiday and vacation programs is averaged out on an hours basis, the average workweek *per year* of American workers is certainly well below the 40 standard.

Basic Factors Affecting Shorter-Hours Trend

This brief survey suggests that three classes of factors have influenced the movement toward shorter hours of work in American industry. The first may be called "social," including the impact of habit and custom. The mores inherited from a primarily agricultural pioneering community undoubtedly contributed to the view, so prevalent during the early years of the struggle for shorter hours, that work was a blessing and that long factory hours were a virtue rather than a vice. Similarly, the mixing in the labor market of immigrants with habits of work inherited from industrially backward nations rendered large masses of the working population relatively indifferent to the shorter-hour movement.

The second factor has been the influence of governmental legislation, both state and federal. Legislative regulation of hours has been of importance, particularly in recent years with NRA, Walsh-Healey, and the Fair Labor Standards Act all contributing substantially to hours reduction. State legislation has been an important factor in reducing the hours of work of women and children.[6]

The third type of factor which has affected the shorter-hour movement is the economic, which may be classified further into four components: (1) the bargaining strength of labor; (2) the bargaining strength of employers; (3) the type of employment; and (4) the general level of economic activity. Thus we have seen that labor in the skilled building trades, by virtue of its strategic bargaining power, has constantly been able to win shorter hours well in advance of the national trend.

The record of particular industries in the movement toward shorter hours is, of course, in large part a reflection of peculiar technological and demand conditions associated with certain types of employment. Thus, one might expect that seasonal industries, where spoilage and other factors require peak production during a relatively short period, would encounter greater difficulty in reducing hours of work than the building industry. And, finally, the recurrence in our industrial development of depression periods with large-scale unemployment has probably tended to organize public opinion behind the shorter-hour movement as a means of reducing unemployment.

The Arguments for Shorter Hours

At various times, the proponents for shorter hours have based their arguments on five principal contentions: (1) The health of the population will be improved by a shorter workweek; (2) the workers, with more free time, will be able to develop into better citizens; (3) shorter hours mean increased leisure, which is not only good in itself but also will permit workers to purchase and enjoy the products of industry; (4) shorter hours will increase worker efficiency enough to offset the loss in worktime; and (5) shorter hours are necessary to ensure full employment. Today the last is the basic area of argument. The arguments as to health are more applicable to a longer workweek than one of 40 hours, except in the cases of particularly dangerous or strenuous occupations. Questions of output and efficiency, once strenuously in contention, are now not vigorously debated.[7] Experiences where hours reduction under 40 have been made—the Kellogg Company, the Akron rubber industry, or the New York City electrical industry—all indicate that efficiency is not materially promoted by reducing hours below 40.[8]

Moonlighting

Hours below 40 seem to spur "moonlighting"—the holding of more than one job. There will always be dual jobholders, but the short workweek appears to have encouraged such activity in Akron, for example, where the six-hour day flourishes.

Moonlighting, by all counts, seems to be an increasing phenomenon.[9] In May 1963, a total of 3.9 million moonlighters were counted by the Bureau of Labor Statistics—an increase of 600,000 over the previous year.[10] Since many moonlighters probably do not report their second activity in order to avoid taxes, or union or employer censure, the actual number is probably greater. A majority of moonlighters is found among professional, self-employed, government employed, education and farming groups, but the increase between 1962 and 1963 was significantly centered among blue-collar workers.

Moonlighting has been attacked as a cause of unemployment. Yet the studies of moonlighters show that the second job held by moonlighters is most often a part-time effort which supplements employment, but does not in itself provide a living; or it is work done by a specialist with a particular skill: a teacher acting as a consultant, a government employed lawyer giving legal counsel, a rubber worker driving a taxi at rush hours, or a New York City electrician wiring houses in his suburban neighborhood on evenings and Saturdays.

But moonlighting is a further indication that the rank and file of labor generally want more income, not shorter hours. As emphasized by a then union research director:

Aside from the workers' desire for their paid holidays and paid vacations there is no evidence in recent experience that workers want shorter *daily* or *weekly* hours. The evidence is all on the other side. Hundreds of local and international officials have testified that the most numerous and persistent grievances are disputes over the sharing of overtime work. The issue usually is not that someone has been made to work, but that he has been deprived of a chance to make overtime pay. Workers are eager to increase their income, not to work fewer hours.[11]

Nevertheless, union officials are persistently seeking fewer hours and less overtime work. The reason is that the pressure from the unemployed is quite different from those employed.

Hours Reduction and Employment

Would shorter hours reduce unemployment? Most economists argue strongly in the negative.[12] They point out the following:

1. Even if basic wage rates are unchanged—that is, if labor is willing to accept wage decreases, unit costs are likely to rise if the workweek is shortened. The need to train personnel, shortages of key skills, additional supervision, and the technical difficulties of work sharing would all be factors. Moreover, in some industries the balance of operations may not be workable with two six-hour shifts instead of one eight-hour one—or, for that matter, there just might not be enough demand for two shifts of 32 or 35 hours where one of 40 hours now suffices. If fewer hours are operated, capital costs per unit rise.

2. Labor's demand, however, involves less hours with no loss of take-home pay. The cost of such a program is charted in Figure 2 and Table 1. Employers are likely to react to such major cost increases as they would to any increase in marginal cost. Prices will tend to rise, a smaller output will be demanded, and ultimately a new equilibrium will be established at a lower level of output. In order to think this through, let us assume that the demand for labor under these circumstances in a particular firm has an elasticity of unity. If the union raises hourly rates 5 per cent and reduces hours of work by 5 per cent, it will have duplicated the readjustment that the employer himself would have made to the changed cost conditions. But since

FIGURE 2.   RISING COST OF SHORTER WORKWEEK

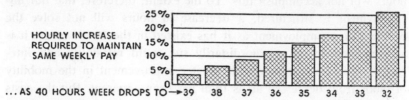

SOURCE: Reprinted by special permission from *Business Week*, October 20, 1962, © 1962 McGraw Hill, Inc. Chart courtesy of Richard D. Irwin, Inc.

a new equilibrium has been established at the higher unit price of labor, there is no incentive to hire any additional labor. It is therefore clear that if the demand curve for labor in a particular firm has an elasticity[13] of unity or greater, as is likely, then the re-employment objective of the shorter-hour movement must fail of accomplishment.

3. Unemployment since 1958 has been heavily concentrated among the unskilled, the young, and the minority groups, as well as in key depressed areas. To find employment for these groups will

TABLE 1

Cost of reduction in workweek
   (a) No loss of pay for employee
   (b) No loss of production for employer
Assume—Rate of pay = $2.00 per hour -
   for 40-hour week—weekly pay = $80.00

(a) If workweek lowered to 35 hours
   No loss of pay for employee
      Hour rate now raised to $2.29 per hour
      to equal $80.00 weekly take-home pay.
      Increase in weekly rate—approximately 14 per cent

(b) If employer requires 40-hour week
   Five hours must be worked overtime
      Time and one-half of $2.29 = $3.44
      35 hours @ $2.29 plus 5 hours @ $3.44 = $97.35
      Increase in weekly rate—28.4 per cent

require great efforts in education and training; but merely reducing hours will not accomplish this. To the extent, therefore, that our unemployment is structured, a decrease in hours will not solve the problem of unemployment as it has existed in the 1960s unless it is accompanied by an extraordinarily successful retraining and integrative program, together with greater improvement in the mobility of labor from depressed areas than has been apparent. But the costs of such programs, combined with the tremendous increase of a shorter workweek (Figure 2 and Table 1), would more likely discourage rather than encourage employment. Dividing up work—and raising its cost—is not likely to improve the matching of jobs and men.

4. Hours reduction would probably not reduce unemployment caused by automation or technological advancement. Automation has created or accentuated employment problems in some areas and among some labor force groups, while building industries and jobs for other areas and groups. The effects of automation, thus, vary considerably from industry to industry, from area to area, and from one labor force group to another.

Moreover, the advent of technological progress and automation does not proceed smoothly throughout industry, but varies widely from industry to industry in its extent and character. A general hours reduction would therefore fall on both heavily and lightly automated industries, on the industries for which technological unemployment is a problem, and on those growing as a result of changing technology. It would give a bonus to the fully employed—or threaten their employment. It would hope, against heavy economic odds, to help those not fully employed.

To succeed in creating employment, a reduction in hours from 40 to 35, with pay maintained, would require a minimum productivity increase of 15 per cent—a most unlikely development indeed. But even if such an increase in productivity occurred, it would probably be insufficient because the substantial investment in expensive equipment required by automation greatly increases fixed costs. To the extent that a shorter workweek keeps this equipment idle, fixed costs per unit during operating periods increase and tend to offset decreases in costs resulting from increases in productivity.

Overtime and Unemployment[14]

In 1964, President Johnson proposed that the rate of overtime be raised in some industries in order to discourage the use of overtime work and to encourage the employment of additional workers instead. Is overtime now more likely to be utilized instead of adding to employment? Organized labor has indicated its belief that it does and has supported a double-time rate to discourage such activity. To understand the problem, one must note what has happened to pay practices, training, and layoff costs in industry.

Fringes, Overtime, and Turnover Costs

There is no doubt that fringe-benefits costs have risen rapidly and substantially. Moreover, fringe benefits such as hospitalization, and many governmental benefits like social security, are employee-related, not hours-related. In addition, state unemployment benefit systems penalize companies with excessive turnover, and hence favor long hours, not more employees.[15]

On the other hand, overtime costs have likewise risen because the base by which time and one-half is figured has risen sharply too. In other words, if a wage is increased from $2.00 to $2.50 per hour, overtime increases from $3.00 to $3.25. Overtime's expense has therefore tended to keep pace with the rise in fringe costs in many industries.

Such a comparison is, however, unrealistic because: (1) It assumes the employer is certain that he knows how long he will need a new employee (or overtime); and (2) it ignores training and layoff costs. The average employer often hesitates to add to the labor force until he feels reasonable assurance that he has need of an employee for a longer period. In the meantime, he will usually use overtime work to fill his needs.

The basic reason for the hesitation to hire is not only the high cost of fringes, but also the high cost of employing and laying off workers. Finding, interviewing, processing, and training people can often cost several hundred dollars per employee. Then if a layoff occurs, new expenses mount. In a large New England plant, each downgrade caused, under the seniority system, three additional ones. The management calculated that the upset, retraining, and lost time cost it $800 per layoff![16] Naturally, this plant hired with caution.

Empirical Evidence

In May 1963, the U.S. Bureau of Labor Statistics found that approximately 22.7 million people, one-third of the labor force, reported workweeks of 41 hours or more.[17] This would seem to confirm the belief of many that limits on overtime pay would be a fertile area to provide jobs for the unemployed—until the statistics are further examined. Then one finds the following:

• One-third of those working long hours were "moonlighters."

• Of the remaining two-thirds (15.2 million), only 4.5 or 29 per cent, received premium pay for hours worked in excess of 40.

• Of those receiving premium pay, less than 60 per cent usually worked long hours.

• In contrast, 85 per cent of those who did not receive premium pay usually worked long hours.

These data also show that those who received overtime pay usually put in only a few hours overtime. Actually, most of those in industry who worked overtime were managers, officials, and proprietors, or professional and technical workers whose work hours were often long as a matter of course, or trade and service or farm workers for whom long hours were typically required at no premium compensation. The authors of this survey concluded:

That only a relatively small proportion of persons working overtime receive premium pay for their extra effort; that those who usually work overtime and who worked very long hours are least likely to receive premium pay; and that even among those occupations and industries where workers are most likely to receive premium pay, the proportion thus compensated is rarely over half of the total number working long hours.[18]

Other studies have found that overtime utilization has not varied substantially within industries over long periods, if adjusted for seasonality, prosperity and the recession, etc.[19] Obviously, therefore, the relation of overtime, fringes, and employment is complex, and employment would not easily be generated by altering this relation.

Concluding Remarks

The hours issue will continue to be a live one, especially if un-employment is not reduced. Basically, an attack on the workweek seems at best a poor remedy for the unemployment problem, which is the real issue in our time.

A second issue is the extent to which reduced hours are to be substituted for economic growth. One of the most careful studies of economic growth has concluded that whereas when the workweek was longer, a reduction in hours would be offset by increases in output per man-hour, this would no longer be true today. Hence a further reduction in hours would reduce economic growth and thereby possibly curtail, not expand, employment.[20]

Again, however, the issue today is unemployment. Unless that problem is overcome, solutions will be sought. The problems and consequences of reducing the workweek as a solution to unemployment, together with related programs and practices, are analyzed in depth in the remaining chapters of this book.

Notes

1. *Encyclopedia of the Social Sciences,* VII (New York: The Macmillan Co., 1932), pp. 480–481.

2. For a more detailed discussion of this point, see Gordon F. Bloom and Herbert R. Northrup, *Economics of Labor Relations,* 5th ed., Homewood, Ill., Richard D. Irwin, Inc., 1965, chap. 17.

3. M. C. Cahill, *Shorter Hours,* New York, Columbia University Press,

1932, pp. 211, 215; and Commission of Inquiry, Inter-Church World Movement, *Report on the Steel Strike of 1919*, New York, 1920, pp. 49, 71.

4. Data from National Industrial Conference Board.

5. See Chap. 2.

6. See Chap. 3.

7. See Chap. 9.

8. For a detailed account of these experiments and their effect on efficiency, see my testimony in *Hours of Work*, Hearings before the Select Subcommittee on Labor of the Committee on Education and Labor, House of Representatives, 88th Cong., 1st Sess., 1964, Part 2, especially pp. 579–588.

9. For a profile of a moonlighter, see Chap. 5.

10. F. A. Bragan and H. R. Hamel, "Multiple Job Holders in May 1963," *Monthly Labor Review*, LXXXVII (March 1964), pp. 249–257.

11. George Brooks, "The History of Organized Labor's Drive for Shorter Hours of Work," *AFL–CIO Conference on Shorter Hours of Work*, published in Special Report No. 1, *Daily Labor Report*, No. 177, September 11, 1956, p. 13.

12. For a detailed analysis of this program, see Chap. 10.

13. Elasticity measures the relationship between the percentage change in quantity divided by the percentage change in price. If the price of labor rises 5 per cent and the employer reduces employment by 5 per cent, the "coefficient of elasticity" is said to be unity, or one. If the percentage change in quantity is greater than the percentage change in price, the elasticity is greater than one, and if the percentage change in quantity is less than the percentage change in price, elasticity is less than one.

14. See Chap. 6 for a theoretical analysis of this question.

15. J. W. Garbarino, "Fringe Benefits and Overtime as Barriers to Expanding Employment," *Industrial and Labor Relations Review*, XVII (April 1964), pp. 426–430.

16. Based on field research by the author.

17. J. E. Blackwood and Carol B. Kalish, "Long Hours and Premium Pay," *July 1963 Monthly Report on the Labor Force*, August 1963, pp. 17–24.

18. *Ibid.*, p. 19.

19. Garbarino, *op. cit.*, pp. 427–432.

20. Edward F. Denison, *The Sources of Economic Growth in the United States and the Alternatives Before Us*, Supplemental Paper, No. 13, New York, Committee for Economic Development, 1962, pp. 40–41.

2. The Influence of Collective Bargaining on Hours

RICHARD L. ROWAN

Department of Industry
Wharton School of Finance and Commerce
University of Pennsylvania

Collective bargaining is one of the several major factors that has influenced the reduction of hours of work in the United States. It can be more accurately termed an "initiator" rather than a "prime mover," however, as the discussion in Chapter 1 implies. Although collective bargaining has resulted in shorter hours for employees in certain instances, it is difficult to show its general effect on hours of work in this country. The record of any specific bargaining situation may reveal the results of negotiations, but to measure the influence beyond the narrow limits of a given case is almost impossible.

Recognizing these difficulties, it is the purpose of this chapter to: (1) present highlights of the unions' drive toward shorter hours; (2) review the thinking of the federation and national unions about shorter hours; (3) examine a few bargaining situations where labor and management have considered the hours question of some importance; and (4) review the trend of hours in relation to vacations and holidays in major collective bargaining agreements.

The Union Movement toward Shorter Hours

Labor unions have sought throughout the past century and a half to reduce the number of hours an employee must work. In their efforts to reach this objective they have used various arguments, running the gamut from shorter hours so that workers may better educate themselves to a reduction in hours in order to provide jobs for more workers.

The Ten-Hour Day

The decade of the 1830s ushered in a period in which American labor made a strong bid for a reduction in hours that normally prevailed from "sun-up to sun-down." Prior to this time, the Mechanics' Union of Trade Associations (1827) and the New York Workingmen's party (1829) had sought a reduction in hours. They had not, however, used strong measures such as the strike to obtain their goals, as was true in the 1830s. The unions' position is reflected in some of the public pronouncements of the day. A statement from a group of Philadelphia journeymen carpenters said: "All men have a just right, derived from their creator to have sufficient time each day for the cultivation of their mind and for self-improvement; Therefore, resolved, that we think ten hours industriously imployed are sufficient for a day's labor."[1] A conservative newspaper in Boston stated further: "Let the mechanic's labor be over when he has wrought ten or twelve hours in the long days of summer, and he will be able to return to his family in season, and with sufficient vigour, to pass some hours in the instruction of his children, or in the improvement of his own mind."[2] Education was the major reason for the desire for shorter hours during the 1830 period. Circulating libraries and the pressures for free, public schools indicated a concern for education as an important element in preparing a person for the responsibilities and duties of citizenship.

Contrary to the stand of the unions, employers thought that a reduction in hours would be detrimental to the workingmen. "To be idle several of the most useful hours in the morning and evening," one newspaper stated, "will surely lead to intemperance and ruin."[3]

Opposition by employers was resisted by the workingmen in the large cities of Baltimore, Boston, and Philadelphia. Groups of workers banded together to make their demands effective through strikes, and in Philadelphia particularly the drive was quite successful. The master cordwainers, master carpenters, and public servants secured a ten-hour day that spread to other employees in the city and to other parts of the country. By the close of the 1830s, the ten-hour day had become a way of life among most artisans and mechanics. The gains of the decade were diminished, however, by the depression of 1837, shortly after President Jackson had established a ten-hour day for shipyard workers in Philadelphia in 1836.

The decade of the 1840s saw a continuation of the drive toward a ten-hour day, but the form of protest from employees was changed beginning with President Van Buren's executive order in 1840 establishing a ten-hour day for all who worked on government projects. Those who sought relief during this period were mainly the unorganized workers in the textile firms in Massachusetts and in other manufacturing areas. Attention was directed toward legislation as a means of coping with the problem, with New Hampshire and Pennsylvania passing ten-hour laws in the late 1840s. The rationale on the part of workers also changed from an education platform to that of an opportunity to do quality work.[4]

The bill signed by President Van Buren in 1840 establishing a ten-hour day for government employees did not spread rapidly to other sectors of the economy. Various groups in the building trades and other crafts secured a ten-hour day by 1845, but the twelve-hour day prevailed in most of American industry until after the Civil War.[5]

The Eight-Hour Day

In the post-Civil War period there was renewed interest in the reduction of hours. A drive toward national organization developed in 1866 when a group of unionists held a convention in Baltimore, attended by seventy-seven delegates, "to create a new unity within the ranks of labor as a whole."[6] The outgrowth of this meeting was the National Labor Union that adopted political and reform measures as its basic *modus operandi*. In an "Address to the Workingmen of the United States," the NLU stated that the eight-hour day was of central importance to all workers. It urged every state to draft a law making it a reality throughout the country. The trend during the 1860s that continued until the 1880s was toward legislative enactment rather than direct action by the unions to gain a shorter working day.

Those who supported an eight-hour day did so for different reasons than those who advocated a ten-hour day. While the latter group concentrated on the health and educational advantages of shorter hours, the eight-hour leaders focused on economic and social objectives of raising wages and the status of workers. These views were enunciated by the champion of the cause of the eight-hour day in the 1860 period, Ira Steward, whose campaign is discussed in Chapter 3.

The movement stimulated by Steward led the federal and state governments to pass legislation making eight hours a legal day's work. This action did not yield concrete results, however, since the laws only applied where "there is no special contract or agreement to the contrary."[7] Such limitations were difficult to overcome as a practical matter and a committee of the National Labor Union reported that "Eight Hour laws have been passed by six states, but for all practical purposes they might as well have never been placed on the statute books, and only can be described as frauds on the laboring class." This experience led the unions to their former position of taking direct action rather than in seeking legislative remedies.

It would be incorrect to suggest that all unions chose to avoid direct action as a means of obtaining an eight-hour day even in the 1860 period. Some groups were not influenced greatly by Steward and the reformers, and they used direct action as a means of achieving their goals. Successful strikes in the textile mills of Eastern Massachusetts and in Pittsfield, Massachusetts, in 1865 led to a reduction of hours. Efforts on the part of ship carpenters and caulkers in New York and Boston have also been reported in the year 1866. With passage in 1867 of various state eight-hour laws came the action on the part of many in the building trades and in the anthracite coal fields to carry out their enforcement.[8]

The Knights of Labor. Direct action in the form of the strike, however, was not looked upon with favor by the dominant national labor organization of the day, the Knights of Labor, although it did engage in strikes from time to time. The first strike in which the Knights became involved over the matter of hours on a national basis was called on July 19, 1883, by the Order of Telegraphers. The strikers were successful with two of the companies in achieving their demands for shorter hours, but the powerful Western Union Company protested vigorously and the employees were forced to go back to work under terms completely unsatisfactory to the union.[9]

The attitude of the Knights was further demonstrated during 1886 when demonstrations were conducted by the Federation of Organized Trades and Labor Unions for an eight-hour day. The Federation had called for the strike but the Knights refused to back it directly. Terence V. Powderly, the leader of the Knights, stated that "no assembly must strike for the eight-hour system on May 1st under the impression they are obeying orders from headquarters. . . ."[10] In spite of Powderly's words many of the members of the Knights of Labor demonstrated. It has been estimated that 340,000 participated in the eight-hour movement and about one-half of them went on strike on May 1, 1886. Gains achieved by about 200,000 workers did not last long. One source estimates that only 15,000 workers were able to keep their gains which had been obtained as a result of direct action. Even though antilabor reaction was partly responsible for labor's lack of success at this time, the ineffective support by the Knights also contributed to its defeat. An incident at the McCormick-Harvester Company in Illinois led to the Haymarket Square affair in May 1886 that adversely affected public sympathy for the eight-hour movement.[11]

The American Federation of Labor. Leadership in the AFL which became firmly established by 1890 reorganized its plans to restore public support for shorter hours. Gompers stated: "We want eight hours, we are determined to have eight hours, we shall try to aid those who are in a condition by May 1, 1890 to obtain eight hours and hope to obtain their assistance in return at some future time. The end of the labor movement, the end of the agitation for the reduction of the hours of labor, will not end in 1890; so long as there is one person seeking employment and cannot obtain it, so long will there be work for our organization."[12] In addition to Gompers' oratory, several tracts were circulated expounding on the "Economic and Social Importance of the Eight-Hour Movement" and "History and Philosophy of the Eight-Hour Movement." Other methods were also used to influence public officials and employers.[13]

Direct action campaigns. Plans were made whereby specific unions would strike at a particular time with backing from others in order to achieve the eight-hour day. The carpenters, miners, granite cutters, and printers were selected to campaign for shorter hours that would apply throughout the industry. Efforts on the part of the carpenters were successful since "the movement established shorter hours for carpenters in 137 cities, and favorably affected 46,197 members of the trade and countless others in various branches of the building trades."[14] Economic conditions did not permit the miners to carry out their plans to strike for an eight-hour day. The granite cutters and printers conducted successful campaigns, but difficulties between the AFL and the national unions caused a change in the approach that was to be followed subsequently by the AFL.

The results of direct action campaigns conducted by various unions with support from the Federation caused a change in the thinking of the leadership of the AFL. After 1891 a new approach was taken that leaned once again in the direction of legislation as a means to secure shorter hours. The opinion on this matter was not unanimous, however, since Gompers was convinced that legislation and government action could not solve this problem for the labor movement. Direct action was the keynote for Gompers who felt that the labor movement should never rely on the government for those things that it could secure for itself. But this point of view was unsatisfactory to those who still worked long hours and realized that direct action had yielded little. Even though Gompers was able to maintain great support for his position, it was clear toward the end of the nineteenth century that legislation would be the primary way in which workers would find relief from their long hours of work.

In the first half of the twentieth century, shorter hours remained a union objective, but few gains were made through direct action or collective bargaining except in particular cases such as basic steel, printing, garment trades, and building trades. Strike activity in 1919 in the steel industry won public support of the shorter-hour movement, and by 1923 the twelve-hour day was abolished in favor of three eight-hour shifts. A similar struggle in the 1920s by the ITU resulted in a 44-hour week.

Significant gains were made as a result of the Fair Labor Standards Act in 1938, which resulted eventually in the statutory workweek of 40 hours. Some industries not covered by FLSA, such as air transport in 1945 and railroads (non-operating employees) in 1949, went on the 40-hour week for the first time.[15] In recent years, unions have sought amendments to the 1938 law, and collective bargaining has worked toward achieving shorter hours through adjustments in vacation time, retirements, holidays, and in the recent "sabbatical leave."

The Federation and the National Unions

A survey of resolutions and policy statements issued by the AFL–CIO and the national unions reveals the thinking of both groups in regard to the most appropriate means of achieving shorter hours. In general terms, several points are made clear: Shorter hours are desirable in order that workers may enjoy more leisure, but, more importantly, in order to alleviate the problems of unemployment; collective bargaining should emphasize the need for shorter hours and each national union should have an organized approach to use at the bargaining table; and unions should attempt to effectuate changes in the Fair Labor Standards Act and to secure other legislation favorable to a reduction in hours.

The AFL–CIO Position

Statements made at conventions of the AFL–CIO provide insight into their thinking on hours of work. In 1957, President George Meany gave an address opening the convention in which he referred to such broad issues as national security, right-to-work laws, and organizing problems. But he did not refer specifically to the hours problem or to collective bargaining as a means of securing a reduction in hours. In referring to many items, he did say: "There is not time to talk about all of these things . . . but just to mention a few there is our problem with automation. . . ."[16] There was no specific discussion of hours as a means of dealing with the problems attendant upon automation and the technologically unemployed. Others noted at the convention that "the subject of hours reduction has been gaining increasing significance. Many unions have been drafting plans for concentrating vigorously on this matter and making workweek reduction a key bargaining issue in the period ahead."[17] The points were made that technical progress should lead to more leisure for workers and the shorter workweek could help maintain employment.

Events that occurred between 1957 and 1959 brought about a new emphasis by the AFL–CIO on the shorter workweek. Advances in technology resulting in unemployment and layoffs during the 1958 recession forced the Federation to take a stronger position.[18] At this time collective bargaining was looked upon as only one of a number of means for reducing hours. "Collective bargaining alone . . . will not achieve adequate hours reductions as rapidly and widely as needed by the economy, for it is proceeding on an industry-by-industry and company-by-company basis."[19] Legislation was deemed a requirement to "meet the overall problem."

In his 1959 presidential address, Meany charged the delegates to resolve "to try to make America stronger . . . by wiping out the cause of unemployment with its degrading consequences. . . ."[20] The delegates responded in a resolution stating that "shorter hours of work must be attained as a vital means of maintaining jobs. . . . We call upon Congress . . . to amend the Fair Labor Standards Act to provide for a seven-hour day and a 35-hour week. The AFL–CIO also urges its affiliated unions to press in collective bargaining for reduction in hours of work with no reduction in take-home pay."[21]

During the 1961 AFL–CIO Convention, Walter Reuther addressed himself to the matter of hours. "They say to us that there is no time to fight for a short work week. We ought to say to them 'We are prepared to work 40 hours a week if you can give every American who wants a job a job at 40 hours,' and if they cannot, then we ought to fight to reduce the level of the work week until every American who is willing and able to work has a job in the American economy."[22] Reuther indicated that the private sector had not generated enough jobs and consequently the government should play an active role in providing relief. He attributed significant responsibility to the government: "The only way that we can be certain that we allocate responsibly our resources and our capabilities is to have a mechanism that deals with this in some kind of a national planning agency." Various means of reducing hours through collective bargaining on such issues as extension of holidays and vacations, early retirement, sabbaticals, and control of overtime were mentioned, but the theme of legislation permeated thinking at the 1961 convention. Collective bargaining was not ruled out altogether as a method of cutting hours, but "public action, principally through legislation, must also be undertaken to provide the most widespread reduction."[23]

In 1963, the AFL–CIO gave recognition to unions which have

been able to secure gains through collective bargaining, commended the Senate Select Subcommittee for holding hearings on hours of work, and further resolved to seek an amendment to the Fair Labor Standards Act in order to provide a 35-hour workweek. The AFL–CIO officers were instructed to aid any affiliate that desired help in bargaining for a reduction of hours by any one of several means, such as increasing time for holidays and vacation, providing for early retirement, and establishing sabbatical leaves.[24]

The National Unions

National unions have advocated several means of reducing hours of work for their members including collective bargaining and legislation. Among these unions, the United Automobile Workers (UAW) and the United Steelworkers (USA) have dealt with hours reduction at length during various conventions.

At recent UAW conventions, resolutions have been passed reaffirming the position that "attainment of a shorter work week is a major collective bargaining goal of our Union."[25] In 1961, at a special collective bargaining convention, the UAW announced that it would explore several approaches to the problem of unemployment, including reduction of the workweek or workday without loss in pay, longer vacations and additional paid holidays, industrial sabbaticals, and early retirement.[26] In addition, Walter Reuther has outlined an approach known as the "flexible adjustment of the workweek," which relates reductions in the workweek to the unemployment rate at a particular time. This program received serious attention at the 1964 convention.[27]

The USA has also spoken of shorter hours as a legitimate union objective. The major thrust has been similar to that of the UAW with emphasis on reduction of hours as a means of coping with unemployment. During the 1958 convention it was recognized that collective bargaining had resulted in improved benefits for the members, but President McDonald reminded the delegates that a unified approach should be taken to the matter of hours. He said: "You cannot be weak and divided if you want to enjoy fewer hours of work per day and per week."[28]

In 1960 the unions' position was that they "must begin progress toward a shorter work week with no reduction in pay"; in 1962 a broader statement noted that "the need to bring about a reduction in hours of work must be met through collective bargaining and through legislative action by amendment of the Fair Labor Standards Act."[29] Specific plans for action were not announced, but it appears that legislative action may hold the greatest promise to the union in reducing the workweek, since a bargain for such with no decrease in wages seems unlikely at the moment.

Direct Action Cases in Collective Bargaining

Even though it is difficult to make a statement on the general effectiveness of collective bargaining on the hours of work, there are cases where direct action has resulted in considerable reductions. Within the past few years there have been at least two dramatic examples where the process of collective bargaining has led directly to a reduction in hours for members of the union: the negotiation of a 25-hour week in the New York City electrical construction industry, and the establishment of industrial sabbaticals in the can and basic steel industries.

The IBEW and the Electrical Contractors

Before a new contract was signed by Local 3 of the IBEW and the electrical contractors in the city of New York in January 1962, construction electricians worked 30 hours a week, six hours a day, at the rate of $4.40 per hour and time and one-half for the seventh hour.[30] Prior to the signing of the new contract, the union had created an artificial shortage of labor in its trade, and contractors had not been able to secure enough construction electricians to perform the work available. Consequently, most members in Local 3 had worked overtime for about five hours a week.[31]

The union took the point of view that "there are five million unemployed. The shorter workweek is the way to give them jobs."[32] Obviously the unemployed were not among the membership of Local 3, but the union took advantage of the general thinking enunciated by the national unions at that time which suggested that shorter hours could cure unemployment. Harry Van Arsdale, business manager of Local 3, indicated that he wanted to "break through the workweek 'barrier' in the construction industry as a safeguard against future unemployment resulting from automation."[33] The New York City strike in 1962 was the first to call for the shorter workweek, in response to the AFL–CIO convention request for all affiliates to push for hours reduction in their collective bargaining during 1962.[34]

Representatives from the 600 electrical contractors viewed the move by the union with skepticism. They maintained that the "shorter workweek was neither warranted nor economically possible." The fact that the union had been forced to bring in about 2,000 construction electricians from other places seemed to be evidence that unemployment was not a problem that the union had to overcome.

In addition to views held by the parties, top government officials stated that a reduction in hours would not be in the public interest. The demands on the nation's productive facilities were thought to be too great to allow shorter hours for employees. President Kennedy, Secretary of Labor Goldberg, Council of Economic Advisors' Chairman Heller, and Secretary of Commerce Hodges were among those who were outspoken over the matter of hours and national goals.[35]

The union did not listen to the admonishments of the government or the arguments of the contractors. Subsequent to a strike of 17 days, the union was able to break the employers' front on January 17 in a settlement with a group of 120 electrical contractors representing approximately 3,000 employees. The terms of the settlement, effective July 1, 1962, were: 25-hour week, 5-hour day, $4.96 an hour wage, and an agreement to permit 2,000 new apprentices in the trade.[36]

The direct action of the union, Local 3, resulted in a major reduction of hours for the members. General union response to this activity, in view of adverse criticism of the federal government, was not favorable. Many union people in national headquarters felt that Van Arsdale had gone too far and that "he had turned the campaign for shorter hours into a joke."[37] But to Van Arsdale it was another success story in his efforts to achieve shorter hours for union members. He had carried the banner for the general seven-hour standard in earlier days, and this was a repeat performance. It is one which serves as a classic example of what a union can achieve in collective bargaining given a certain set of circumstances.

The USA and the Basic Steel and Can Industries

During 1962 the USA and representatives of the American Can Company and the Continental Can Company entered into two-year contracts establishing industrial sabbaticals for their employees. In 1963 an agreement was reached between the union and representatives of the basic steel industry resulting in similar benefits to workers. For the first time in American industrial relations, the collective bargaining process enforced shorter hours for union members through the sabbatical leave.

Consistent with the thinking of the day in trade union circles, the USA announced that the approach would help solve general unemployment problems. "We recommend this (extended vacation agreement) to American labor and to American industry as another method of trying to solve the problems of unemployment."[38] In dealing with the can companies, the union realized that job security was more important to the workers than wage increases. This permitted it to bargain for an hours reduction without achieving a wage increase. The companies had insisted that labor costs could not be increased since they had been seriously affected by competition in packaging materials. Earlier bargaining in basic steel had also indicated some receptivity to the idea of extended vacations or sabbaticals and the union was ready to press the idea harder in negotiating with the can companies.

The can companies negotiated together a contract with the union with the following provisions: An employee with 15-years seniority will be entitled to three months of paid vacation or sabbatical leave time every five years; an employee's regular vacation time will be included in the year the sabbatical is taken. Thus a worker with 15 years service will have three weeks of regular vacation each year and every fifth year an extra two months-plus of sabbatical leave.[39]

On June 17, 1963, the USA and the basic steel companies entered into an agreement that established a sabbatical program. It provides a three-month vacation with pay every five years for one-half of the hourly paid workers. Only the top half of all hourly paid workers regardless of years of service in each company will be affected by this agreement. In the basic steel industry, approximately 50 per cent of the hourly paid employees have 15 years of service while some 22.6 per cent have 10 to 15 years. The experience, however, will vary widely from one company to the next.[40] It is estimated that 40,000 production and maintenance workers will have three months off in 1964. David McDonald predicted that some 20,000 to 25,000 jobs will be added in basic steel as a result of the sabbatical programs, thus reaffirming his position that shorter hours can serve as an effective weapon against unemployment.[41]

Trends in Vacations and Holidays

One of the most interesting developments in labor relations during the past few decades has been the significant increase in payments to employees for time not worked. These payments have occurred, in addition to the sabbaticals mentioned earlier, in the form of vacations and holidays. Collective bargaining undoubtedly has had more impact on hours reduction via this route than through an actual shortening of hours worked per week. Peter Henle reports that:

A review of the changes in paid leisure between 1940 and 1960 shows that there was no major shift in the standard workweek. Perhaps the most significant development was that more than half the total gain in paid leisure resulted from increased vacation and holiday time, rather than a reduction in working hours.[42]

Even though this statement covers the organized and unorganized sectors of the labor force, BLS reports for the years 1940 and 1957, covering the organized sector, seem to substantiate the claim that collective bargaining has had a considerable influence on vacation and holiday time for union members.

Vacations

In 1940 some two million organized wage earners had contracts granting them vacations with pay. This represented about one-fourth of all union members at that time. A majority of the workers mentioned had a vacation period of one week and rarely more than two weeks. In a few cases an employee would have a two-week vacation when certain specifications, such as length of service, were met. By 1957, the picture had changed considerably and 91 per cent of all union members were eligible for vacations with pay. About 84 per cent of all agreements in 1957 provided for at least three weeks of vacation for longer service employees.

BLS studies covering collective bargaining provisions specifying vacation time are not available after 1957, but Henle has prepared data relevant to plant and office personnel and vacations. He notes that in 1961, 25 per cent of all plant personnel were eligible for four weeks of vacation after 25 years of service, and 29 per cent were eligible for three weeks after 10 years of service, and two to three years was the service requirement for two weeks.[43]

Holidays

Paid holiday time also has been a major concern of the union in collective bargaining. Before World War II, holidays without pay seemed to be the common practice of most employers. The practice changed somewhat during the war, but a BLS report states that:

Although an increasing number of union agreements make provision for paying wage earners for some or all of the major holidays, the majority of agreements in manufacturing, construction, and mining merely provide time off on holidays, without pay.[44]

By 1958, however, only 12 per cent of workers covered under collective bargaining agreements were not entitled to paid holidays and over 60 per cent were entitled to seven holidays or more. Henle estimates that in 1961 almost 95 per cent of plant workers received pay for holidays not worked. Some 7 per cent were given nine or more paid holidays with the average being seven holidays with pay. Agreements have been made which grant days off in addition to the regular holiday in order to give the employee a longer weekend or more leisure. For example, the Friday after Thanksgiving or a day preceding or following Christmas day have been written into some agreements.

A later BLS study covering paid-holiday provisions in major collective bargaining agreements in 1961 concludes that nine out of ten contracts studied contain provisions for paid holidays. The statistics reveal also that the percentage of collective bargaining agreements granting nine days and over increased from 9 per cent in 1958 to 11 per cent in 1961.[45]

Conclusions

The research conducted to determine the influence of collective bargaining on the hours of work leads to several conclusions:

1. Collective bargaining prior to the twentieth century had only a minimal, if any, effect on the hours of work for employees. Campaigns conducted by the unions during the drives for a ten-hour day and the eight-hour day enlisted public sympathy for a reduction in hours, but the impact was not felt at the bargaining table. It was legislation that brought relief to those who campaigned for shorter hours. President Van Buren signed an executive order in 1840 establishing a ten-hour day for all who worked on government projects, and a few states passed laws in the 1860s granting an eight-hour day in cases where "there is no special contract or agreement to the contrary."

The special qualifying clauses in regard to the eight-hour laws encouraged unions to take direct action with employers in an effort to obtain their goals, but they met with little success. Some results were obtained through strikes by those who worked in the textile mills in Eastern Massachusetts and as ship carpenters and caulkers in New York.

2. After the turn of the century, unions continued to push for shorter hours through collective bargaining. In some cases such as basic steel, printing, garment trades, and building trades, the objective was reached. But it was not until 1938 that a general reduction of hours was established with the passage of the Fair Labor Standards Act that finally resulted in a statutory workweek of 40 hours.

3. During recent decades, the national unions and federations have emphasized the necessity of collective bargaining as a means of reducing hours of work, but the major thrust has been to repeal the Fair Labor Standards Act.

4. In collective bargaining there have been a few notable examples where the union has been able to obtain a reduction in the hours of work. The success of Local 3, IBEW, in seeking a 25-hour week in New York City, and the establishment of sabbatical leaves in the can and basic steel industries by the United Steelworkers are examples of what a union can do through bargaining given certain circumstances.

5. In the future, unions will seek a reduction in hours at the bargaining table through such means as sabbatical leaves, early retirements, and extended vacations and holidays. Reductions in the basic workweek will not be achieved generally by collective bargaining and not through legislation in the foreseeable future with a government disposed against it.

Notes

1. Foster Rhea Dulles, *Labor in America,* New York, Thomas Y. Crowell, 1954, p. 60.
2. *Ibid.,* p. 61.
3. *Ibid.*
4. *Ibid.,* pp. 84–85. (Dulles reports that the "average working day in the textile factories ranged from 11 hours and 24 minutes to 13 hours and 31 minutes according to the season.")

5. Gordon F. Bloom and Herbert R. Northrup, *Economics of Labor Relations*, 4th ed., Homewood, Ill., Richard D. Irwin, Inc., 1961, p. 584.

6. Dulles, *op. cit.*, p. 100.

7. *Ibid.*, p. 108.

8. Marion Cotter Cahill, *Shorter Hours: A Study of the Movement Since the Civil War*, New York, Columbia University Press, 1932, pp. 142–143.

9. *Ibid.*, pp. 149–150.

10. Dulles, *op. cit.*, p. 146.

11. Cahill, *op. cit.*, p. 156.

12. Gompers to Edward Plant, December 21, 1889, as quoted in Philip Taft, *The AF of L in the Time of Gompers*, New York, Harper & Bros., 1957, pp. 142–143.

13. Cahill, *op. cit.*, p. 160.

14. Taft, *op. cit.*, p. 144.

15. Bloom and Northrup, *op. cit.*, pp. 585–586.

16. AFL–CIO, *Proceedings of the Second Constitutional Convention*, Atlantic City, New Jersey, December 5–12, 1957, I, p. 13.

17. *Ibid.*, II, p. 145.

18. AFL–CIO, *Proceedings of the Third Constitutional Convention*, San Francisco, California, September 17–23, 1959, II, pp. 95–96.

19. *Ibid.*, I, p. 640.

20. *Ibid.*, p. 26.

21. *Ibid.*, p. 641.

22. AFL–CIO, *Proceedings of the Fourth Constitutional Convention*, Miami Beach, Florida, December 7–13, 1961, I, p. 377.

23. *Ibid.*, pp. 560–561.

24. AFL–CIO, *Proceedings of the Fifth Constitutional Convention*, New York, New York (November 1963), as quoted in *Hours of Work*, Hearings before the Select Subcommittee on Labor of the Committee on Education and Labor, House of Representatives, 88th Cong., 1st Sess., part II, pp. 525–527.

25. UAW, *Proceedings of the 17th Constitutional Convention*, Atlantic City, New Jersey, October 9–16, 1959, pp. 571–572.

26. UAW, *Proceedings of the Special Collective Bargaining Convention*, Detroit, Michigan, April 27–29, 1961, p. 106.

27. UAW, *Report of Walter P. Reuther to the 19th UAW Constitutional Convention*, Atlantic City, New Jersey, March 20–27, 1964, p. 72.

28. USA, *Proceedings of the Ninth Constitutional Convention*, Atlantic City, New Jersey, 1958, p. 10.

29. USA, *Proceedings of the Eleventh Constitutional Convention*, Miami Beach, Florida, September 17–21, 1962, p. 299.

30. *The New York Times*, January 3, 1962, p. 1.

31. *Fortune*, LXV (March 1962), p. 189.

32. *Ibid.*

33. *The New York Times*, January 9, 1962, p. 24.

34. A. H. Raskin, "If We Had a 20-Hour Week," *New York Times Magazine*, February 4, 1962, p. 15.

35. *Ibid.*

36. *The New York Times*, January 18, 1962, p. 1, and *Business Week* (January 27, 1962), p. 36.

37. A. H. Raskin, "No 25-Hour Week for Him," *The New York Times Magazine*, March 18, 1962, p. 57.
38. *Business Week*, October 13, 1962, p. 108.
39. *Ibid.*, pp. 106–108.
40. *Business Week*, February 8, 1964, p. 70.
41. *Business Week*, June 22, 1963, p. 23.
42. Peter Henle, "Recent Growth of Paid Leisure for U. S. Workers," *Monthly Labor Review*, LXXXV (March 1962), p. 257; see also "Vacation with Pay in Union Agreements, 1940," *Monthly Labor Review*, November 1940, pp. 1070–1077; "Paid Vacation Provisions in Major Union Contracts," BLS, Bulletin 1233, 1958.
43. *Ibid.*, pp. 253–254.
44. *Ibid.*, p. 254, and "Vacations and Holiday Provisions in Union Agreements," *Monthly Labor Review*, May 1943, p. 929; "Paid Holidays in Major Contracts," *Monthly Labor Review*, January 1959, pp. 26–32.
45. James A. Socknat, "Prevalence of Holiday Provisions in Major Union Contracts, 1961," *Monthly Labor Review*, LXXXV (May 1962), pp. 522–527.

3. The Influence of Legislation on Hours

R<small>AY</small> M<small>ARSHALL</small>

Department of Economics
The University of Texas

In outlining the history of hours legislation, we shall discuss the opposition to shorter hours during the nineteenth century, the reasons for the early agitation for shorter hours, and the nature of past and present hours legislation.

Opposition to Shorter Hours

The most obvious reason for the importance of shorter hours during the 1830s was the length of the working day. Employers saw nothing wrong with urban workers following the agricultural working day of from "sun to sun." The longer working day was accepted by the public because it was the norm for employers, merchants, and retail clerks, and because of a prevailing, almost religious, conviction of the virtues of hard work.

Employers usually couched their arguments against shorter hours in terms of the general welfare. In 1822, for example, master builders in Boston considered the carpenters' demand for a ten-hour day "fraught with numerous and pernicious evils," because "altering the time of commencing and terminating their daily labor, from that which has been customary from time immemorial" would have an "unhappy influence" on apprentices "by seducing them from the course of industry and economy of time," and would expose the journeymen themselves "to many temptations and improvident practices" from which they were "happily secure" when working from sun to sun.[1] The Boston employers also hinted broadly at the foreign origin of the ten-hour agitation. They were convinced that this movement did not originate with "any of the faithful and industrious Sons of New England . . . the early rising and industry of whose inhabitants are universally proverbial. . . ."[2] Similar sentiments were voiced by the "gentlemen engaged in building" who employed the master builders. These gentlemen were particularly concerned that the ten-hour movement might spread

to and embrace all the Working Classes in every department in Town and Country, thereby effecting a most injurious change in all modes of business, and in the operations of agriculture and commerce opening a wide door for idleness and vice, and finally commuting the present condition of the Mechanical Classes, made happy and prosperous by frugal, orderly, temperate and ancient habits, for that degraded state, by which in other countries, many of these classes are obliged to leave their homes, bringing with them their feelings and habits, and a spirit of discontent and insubordination to which our native mechanics have hitherto been strangers.

While employers continued to use such arguments against shorter hours, public officials seem to have relied more on the argument that such regulations, especially as they related to adult males, abridged individual freedoms. In Massachusetts, for example, a legislative investigating committee refused to recommend a ten-hour bill in 1845 because, while they agreed "with the petitioners in their desire to lessen the burthens imposed upon labor," they differed as to the "means by which these burthens are sought to be removed." The Committee looked for improvement "in the progressive improvement in art and science, in a higher appreciation of man's destiny in less love for money, and more ardent love for social happiness and intellectual superiority."[3]

More specifically, the legislation was opposed because it might drive industry to other states, would necessitate wage reductions, and since "labor is on an equality with capital, and indeed controls it, it is intelligent enough to make its own bargains, and look out for its own interests without any interference from us."[4] In 1847 a committee to investigate the feasibility of a ten-hour law in New Hampshire reported that

a proper reduction in the hours of labor would be found advantageous to all parties. Employers would realize a greater profit, even in less time, from labourers more vigorous and better able to work, from having had suitable time to rest; while the operatives would be allowed that time for intellectual and moral culture, which duty to themselves and others most imperatively demands.[5]

In spite of this attitude, the majority report refused to recommend legislation, calling instead for voluntary action by employers.

While legislatures were willing to relax their laissez-faire ideas to regulate the hours of women and children, many employers and courts opposed even this legislation. In Massachusetts, some employers argued against an eight-hour law for children under 16 years of age on the grounds that "either the machinery and the adults must stop at the end of eight hours or we must discharge the children."[6] The textile manufacturers regarded the employment of children "as a necessity to the building up and maintaining of a competent and adequate labor force for the textile industry," because it was "essential that the textile operative should begin his career in the mill at an early age . . . if he does not begin before 16 he has either come to look down on mill work or is an indifferent learner."[7] Moreover, many believed that "the hand must be trained to the proper dexterity during the muscle-forming years, else the operative will always be clumsy and sluggish."[8] In 1895, the Illinois Supreme Court, in a widely quoted decision, held that the police powers of a state could not be used to deny women their "fundamental and inalienable right of freedom of contract."[9]

However, while the "freedom to contract" principle continued to hold for men, the U.S. Supreme Court upheld a 1903 Oregon statute limiting the hours of women to ten in mechanical establishments, laundries, and factories.[10] This was not special legislation, according to the Court, because "healthy mothers are essential to vigorous offspring." Similarly, the Court upheld an 1896 Utah law which prohibited employment for more than eight hours per day in underground mines, smelters, and ore-reduction workers. The Court held that

While the general experience of mankind may justify us in believing that men may engage in ordinary employment more than eight hours per day without injury to their health, it does not follow that labor for the same length of time is innocuous when carried on beneath the surface of the earth, where the operative is deprived of fresh air and sunlight, and is frequently subjected to foul atmosphere and a very high temperature, or to the influence of noxious gases generated by the process of refining or smelting.[11]

In 1905, however, the Supreme Court declared unconstitutional a New York law which, among other things, limited the hours of work in bakery and confectionary shops to ten a day.[12] The majority ruled in that case that ". . . To the common understanding, the trade of baker has never been regarded as an unhealthy one." Therefore, "Statutes of the nature of that under review, limiting hours in which grown and intelligent men may labor to earn their living are mere meddlesome interferences with the rights of an individual."

The Shorter-Hour Movements

These laissez-faire ideas concerning the desirability of social legislation obviously were better suited to agricultural than industrial societies. Industrialization almost invariably created worker dissatisfaction, and the United States' experience was by no means unique:

Industrialization characteristically redesigns and reshapes its human raw materials, whatever the source. It transforms urban populations of old commercial cities; it transplants peasants, farmers, and tribal groups to mines, factories, and offices, and it imports labor into empty regions and countries. The development of an industrial work force necessarily involves the destruction of old ways of life and work and the acceptance of the new imperatives of the industrial work place and community. The drastic changes in human beings and their relationships required to achieve a settled industrial work force have been made only with significant reactions from the workers-in-process. While the work force has in the end been malleable, the metamorphosis has ordinarily involved considerable stress and tension and even violence.[13]

The earliest form of that protest in the United States involved class arguments over equal citizenship. The workers' earliest demands for shorter hours were

. . . closely related to their status as citizens of a democracy. . . . work from "sun to sun" was held to be incompatible with citizenship, for it did not afford the workman the requisite leisure for the consideration of public questions and therefore condemned him to an inferior position in the state.[14]

There were many other reasons why the early protest movement in America should have rejected agrarian ideas with respect to hours of work:

1. It became increasingly obvious that those ideas were not suited to the urban environment. Women who worked in factories threatened their health more than had been the case on the farm. Children also needed more and different education in an industrial society. Moreover, the attitude toward work was undoubtedly different. Agricultural workers (and shopkeepers, employers, and professionals) tend to be individualistic because their work is such that they usually set their own pace, and barring natural disasters, there is a direct relationship between hard work and benefits. For the industrial hourly wage worker, on the other hand, there is frequently no such obvious relationship.

2. Many leaders of the early protest movements in America were immigrants whose class attitudes were molded by European conditions. But some immigrants were also unhappy because their hours were actually longer in America than they had been in Europe.[15]

3. Moreover, the working day for urban workers who worked from "sun to sun" was actually longer than for agricultural workers because of the longer time required for the urban worker to travel to the job.

4. Finally, while early protest movements centered on equal citizenship arguments for shorter hours, as industrialization proceeded shorter hours were demanded as a means of combating unemployment. Increasing technology suggested that workers should and could have shorter hours because it required less time to produce a given output.

But although these factors produced demands for shorter hours, they do not explain why this objective should be achieved through legislation. Employers might voluntarily see the need for shorter hours, which they were told might increase output and sales by reducing fatigue and increasing the workers' leisure time to enjoy more products. While a few employers accepted this argument, most of them were persuaded that whether you paid by the piece or by the day, the longer the hours the shorter the pay, and therefore the lower the cost per unit of output (especially where fixed costs were high and wages were low) and the higher the profits. It was, moreover, competitively difficult for individual employers to initiate movements for shorter hours.

Collective bargaining was another alternative which was actually tried during these early years but proved ineffective, because workers had greater political than bargaining rights during the 1830s and 1840s, legislation could be secured faster and was broader in coverage than collective bargaining contracts, and the intellectuals who participated in these early hours movements favored legislation for ideological reasons.

The Ten-Hour Movement

Isolated strikes for the ten-hour day in various Eastern cities during 1833–1834 were followed in 1835 by a general movement.[16] The chief argument for the ten-hour day at this time continued to be the need for leisure to attain equal citizenship, but was supplemented by the contention that long hours were injurious to health and led to alcoholism—though the latter argument seems mainly to have been advanced to answer the employers' traditional charges that shorter hours would lead to "idleness and debauchery."[17] The various mechanics' societies supporting the ten-hour movement also argued that shorter hours would lead to "equal, if not a greater amount of labour, with less animal exhaustion than could be expected under the 'day break to dark night system.' "[18]

These movements were so successful that by 1840 most of the skilled trades had achieved the ten-hour day in Eastern cities and towns. Government and factory workers had greater difficulty achieving the shorter workday, though in those places where the skilled trades won the ten-hour day, municipalities generally reduced hours for their workers. The federal government offered greater resistance, but in 1840, after Congress repeatedly refused to pass a ten-hour law, the National Trades' Union succeeded in getting President Van Buren to issue an executive order establishing the ten-hour day on all government works.

These efforts were followed during the 1840s by attempts to get legislation establishing the ten-hour day for all workers. Efforts by the New England Working Men's Association to get ten-hour legislation in various New England states bore fruit in 1847 when New Hampshire passed the first ten-hour law. However, the law proved ineffective because it permitted workers to contract for longer hours. It was hoped that this concession to the freedom-to-contract forces would have the effect of limiting hours, but employers used their superior bargaining power to extract contracts for over ten hours. Similar laws were passed in Pennsylvania (1848), Maine (1848), Rhode Island (1851), and Connecticut (1855). In 1852 Ohio enacted a law providing that children under fourteen should not be permitted, and women and minors under 18 could not be forced, to work more than ten hours a day. In 1853, New York established by law, in the absence of contracts, the ten-hour day for public work. In 1851, California passed a law making ten hours a legal day "in any action in law." The length of the workday in the South at this time is suggested by the fact that in 1853 Georgia became the first Southern state to pass an hours law when it provided that for "all white persons under twenty-one years of age, in all cotton woolen and other manufacturing establishments or machine shops the legal day should be 'from sunrise to sunset, the usual and customary time for meals being allowed.' "[19] During the 1850s, the strength of trade unionism and the ineffectiveness of the ten-hour laws, caused labor organization to turn to "direct action" instead of agitation for legislation. In Massachusetts, however, where unions were weak, the New England Industrial League continued to press for legislation.[20]

The Eight-Hour Movements

The depression following the end of the Civil War gave rise to renewed demands for hours legislation. The eight-hour day had been established in a few places before that time, the earliest authentic case having been in the Charlestown, Massachusetts, navy yard in 1842, but it was not until Ira Steward, the Boston Machinist, gave the movement a philosophy that it really became a "national" movement. Steward rejected the wages-fund theory that wages were governed by the amount of capital available to pay wages to the laboring population. He argued that wages were determined by the habits, customs, and wants of the working classes. Ricardo, Marx, and the classical economists also thought wages were determined by customary subsistence; but they, unlike Steward, were relatively pessimistic about the ability to change the worker's habits and customs, especially those which controlled the population. Steward, on the other hand, felt that change could be brought about by a general eight-hour law for all workers. He reasoned that workers could take advantage of the surplus produced by advancing technology to shorten hours. Since wages depended on wants, reducing hours and increasing wants would increase wages. An eight-hour law would be superior to trade union action because it would cause weaker workers to increase their wants and demand higher wages, thus preventing them from undermining the standards of the stronger workers. Rising wages would lead to greater use of machines, increasing the surplus, starting the whole cycle over again. Steward also felt that rising wages would reduce nonwage incomes and gradually lead to a cooperative commonwealth.[21]

Steward's program to achieve eight-hour legislation required extensive publicity and education to influence public opinion. To achieve this objective, eight-hour leagues were established throughout the country which were almost as extensive as trade unions. Moreover, the National Labor Union, established in 1866, made eight-hour legislation its principal objective and rejected traditional trade union and strike activity. As a result of this agitation, eight-hour laws were passed in Illinois, Wisconsin, Connecticut, Missouri, and New York in 1867 and in California in 1868. Similar laws were defeated in Pennsylvania, Michigan, Maryland, and Minnesota. As with the earlier ten-hour laws, however, these statutes proved ineffective because they contained no enforcement provisions and permitted contracts for longer hours. When Governor R. E. Fenton of New York was asked to issue a proclamation that employers observe the law, he replied: "It would be an act of unwarranted assumption to issue a proclamation requiring its observance."[22] Unions made weak and unsuccessful attempts to enforce these statutes by strikes.

The eight-hour law for federal employees passed in 1868 met a similar fate. Federal officials either refused to enforce the law or insisted that a reduction in hours be accompanied by a reduction in wages. Federal officials also disregarded President Grant's 1869 directive that wages not be reduced when hours were cut.[23] However, in May 1872, President Grant prohibited by proclamation any reduction in wages when hours were reduced, and Congress passed a law restoring back pay to those who had lost wages. Even after this, however, the law was ineffective because it was not enforced, and a Supreme Court decision in 1876 permitted the government to make longer contracts with its employees.[24] While Perlman observed that "the expectations of the workingmen that the Federal law would blaze the way for the eight-hour system in private employment failed to materialize," he called the federal law "an important landmark," because it "demonstrated to the wage earners that, provided they concentrated on a modest object and kept up steady pressure, their prospects for success were not entirely hopeless, hard as the road may seem to travel."[25]

Attitude of the AFL

While the American Federation of Labor declared in favor of shorter hours, it generally opposed legislation for this purpose except for women, children, government workers, and those in certain hazardous occupations.[26] There were, however, numerous debates on this subject at AFL conventions, especially in 1913 and 1914.[27] The state federations, the functions of which were principally legislative and which represented the interests of weaker unions unable to attain shorter hours through "direct action," were leaders of the minority favoring eight-hour legislation. As a result of the AFL's position, and other opposition to labor legislation, the movement for general eight-hour legislation came to an end until the New Deal period. Indeed, even the movement to get laws for special groups was slowed considerably, in spite of the Supreme Court's favorable decision in the Bunting case. No state attempted a general hours law between 1917 and 1933.[28]

Legislation for Special Groups

Most of the legislative efforts of labor unions after the formation of the AFL involved special groups. Agitation for enforcement of legislation covering federal employees led to the 1888 eight-hour law for workers in the Government Printing Office and the Post Office Department.[29] An 1892 law provided the eight-hour day for government employees and government contractors. However, this law, like its predecessors, was emasculated by narrow interpretations, lack of enforcement, and Congressional exemptions. It was not until 1908, when the President issued an executive order commanding enforcement of the law, and 1912, when Congress passed a more stringent measure, that serious efforts were made to enforce the eight-hour law in federal employment. In 1907 Congress made 16 hours the maximum workday on interstate railroads.

The most spectacular movement for the eight-hour day came in 1916, when the railroad brotherhoods succeeded in forcing Congress to pass the Adamson Act, which provided for the eight-hour day with time and one-half for overtime for operating railroad employees. The brotherhoods created an emergency by threatening to strike at a time of international crisis. The provisions of the Adamson Act were temporarily extended to other railroad workers during the war when the government took over and ran the railroads.

By 1889, nineteen states had passed laws limiting the hours of children. In 1903 Illinois passed the first eight-hour law for children and from then on many states passed similar legislation. The 1913 Massachusetts law was particularly important because it was the first such law in an important textile state. Some kind of child labor law existed in ever state by 1961. Sixteen states and Puerto Rico limited to 40 the weekly hours of children under 16 years of age. Most states provided that children under 16 could not work longer than eight hours a day or 48 hours a week.

The first ten-hour law for women was passed by Ohio in 1852 and the first enforceable law was enacted by Massachusetts in 1879. By 1920 maximum hour laws for women had been enacted in 43 states, the District of Columbia, and Puerto Rico. In 1960, only nine states had no maximum hour laws for women, 18 states limited hours to eight or less a day, 14 set nine hours as a maximum, and 11 permitted no more than 10 hours.[30]

Hours legislation for women and children was much more effective than the laws regulating men's hours before the Fair Labor Standards

Act (FLSA) of 1938. This was true not only because most of the states seem to have enforced the women's and children's provisions with greater care, but also because these laws provided limitations on hours while the regulations for men established standard hours which could be exceeded either by contract or by the payment of overtime rates. A 1928 study by the U.S. Women's Bureau, for example, examined intensively a large number of establishments in industries with large concentrations of women employees in nine states and concluded that the laws were important causes of reducing the hours of women.[31] The study also revealed that the hours laws had little effect on employment of women.

By 1933, there were the following numbers and classifications of laws covering the hours of men:

1. General declaratory, or "legal day's work" laws—permitting contracts for longer hours—17 states
2. Public works laws—27 states, federal government and territories
3. Railroad laws—27 states and federal government
4. Street railway laws—12 states
5. Bus drivers' laws—7 states
6. Mining laws—16 states, federal government and Alaska
7. Laws covering special miscellaneous occupations—19 states.[32]

A particularly important law establishing ten hours for most men in mills, factories, or manufacturing establishments was enacted in Oregon in 1913. This law permitted overtime, but not to exceed three hours a day. The Act was based on the premise that working over ten hours a day was "injurious to the physical health and well-being of such person, and tends to prevent him from acquiring that degree of intelligence that is necessary to make him a useful and desirable citizen of the state." The Oregon Supreme Court upheld this law as a valid exercise of that state's police powers and was sustained by the U.S. Supreme Court in the 1917 Bunting decision.[33] In

that decision the Court ignored its 1905 Lochner decision and implied
that no constitutional question was raised where states limited hours
as a means of protecting their citizens' health. Since this decision,
moreover, the Supreme Court has not questioned the states' right to
regulate the hours of labor.

New Deal Legislation

The depression of the 1930s caused new demands for federal
legislation regulating the hours of work. Even the AFL advocated
a national 30-hour week as a means of combating unemployment.
The codes of fair competition permitted by the National Industrial
Recovery Act of 1933 all provided for limitations on hours. While
the results of the NRA codes are far from conclusive, they give
important clues concerning the influence of legislation on hours and
employment. The results of the FLSA have been obscured by the
fact that it came at a time of greater recovery from the depression
and much of our experience with that law has been during relatively
prosperous times. Moreover, unlike the FLSA, the NRA codes
usually established *maximum* rather than *standard* hours.

The NRA was based on the theory that shorter hours would
spread employment and stimulate the economy by increasing purchasing power. This idea was endorsed by the AFL, which argued
that even though shorter hours would have the effect of raising wages
and costs, total costs would increase by less than the increase in
wages, depending on the ratio of labor costs to total costs.[34] With
respect to the NRA's experience, however, Roos concluded that the
Administration was successful in spreading employment, but "that
one must bend over backwards to say that the NRA helped employment throughout industry. While employment has risen since the
NRA was first conceived, most of the increase actually occurred
before codes were adopted and at the best the pre-code gains have
been maintained. In view of the uncertainties arising from codes and
the jerky stimulating and retarding effects, it now seems reasonable

to conclude that the NRA did not aid economic recovery in the United States."[35] Charles R. Roos argued that the codes introduced unnecessary rigidities in the use of skilled workmen by inflexible maximum-work-period rules. These rigidities made it difficult to use skilled manpower effectively and thus interfered with the employment of unskilled manpower. Moreover, according to Roos, because of differences in wage rates and the ratios of wages to value added, displacements and disparities were created by the application of "a shortening-to-uniform-hours, no-wage reduction program" to all industries.[36] However, the fact that the capital goods industries, which had relatively high ratios of wages to value added, were operating at hours much below those established by the codes softened the impact of these disparities. Roos concluded, therefore,

. . . that mandatory shorter hours, on a basis which reduces them proportionately in all nondurable-consumers'-goods industries and services, can be applied profitably once during a depression to prevent needless further declines in wages in such industries and to increase the demand for machinery. But the changes must not be drastic and must be confined to the industries named. If the shorter hours are forced also upon the durable-goods industries (capital and consumers') the net result will be much less favorable and may even be harmful.[37]

Roos's statistics fail to support his conclusion that the NRA did not influence total employment. To be sure, there were increases in employment in most industries *before* the codes went into operation, but since they apparently were in anticipation of the codes, it is difficult to see why these increases should not be attributed to the NRA. Of course, much of the difficulty here, as in a great deal of the empirical work in economics, is in determining what might have been if the NRA had not been adopted.

The NRA was declared unconstitutional in 1935, but the following year the Walsh-Healey Public Contracts Act was passed to provide minimum standards for federal contractors producing goods of value in excess of $10,000. The Walsh-Healey Act provides that no employee working on these contracts may be employed for more than eight hours in any one day or 40 hours in any one week unless such employee is paid time and one-half for overtime. Walsh-Healey, unlike the FLSA, requires overtime payments on a daily or weekly basis, whichever is greater.

While the FLSA provides for a number of exemptions, as amended in 1961, it establishes a minimum wage of $1.25 per hour; time and one-half pay for overtime after 40 hours a week, applied in stages to workers newly covered in 1961 with the final stage reached September 3, 1965; and a minimum age of 16 for general employment. The FLSA was upheld in 1941 by the U.S. Supreme Court as a valid exercise of the federal power to regulate interstate commerce.[38] The law applies to all workers in interstate commerce or in the production of goods for interstate commerce.

The recent agitation by the AFL–CIO and other forces to combat unemployment by increasing overtime penalties and shortening hours has led to a number of proposals to amend the FLSA. Among the bills introduced in the 88th Congress, for example, were: HR 355, which specified that one year after enactment 32 hours would become the point after which pay of at least time and one-half would take effect; HR 3102, which provided that two years following enactment overtime of at least time and one-half would become applicable after 37.5 hours, and that two years later the hours standard would fall to 35; and HR 1680, which provided that in certain industries (recommended by tripartite committees) the overtime rate after 40 hours would be raised from time and one-half to double time. Hearings were held on these measures but the bills did not advance beyond the committee stage.

Summary and Conclusions

The earliest manifestation of organized labor protest over hours in the United States obviously had broader implications. The hours movements at first took the form of demands for equal citizenship.

Later, however, other arguments were emphasized, including the need to share the work and take advantage of increased productivity from technological change; to protect the health and safety of children, women, and men engaged in hazardous occupations; to raise wages by increasing the workers' standards of living; and to increase productivity by reducing fatigue. Hours legislation for government workers was supported by the labor movement because government employees could not use "direct action" and because it was assumed that private employers would follow the government's examples.

Opposition to shorter hours came from many sources. Employers frequently argued that reducing hours would degrade the workers' morals. Employers and legislators also argued that these laws would create competitive disadvantages for those states which passed them. But the most important objections to shorter hours, at least of those openly advanced, involved freedom of contract. This perhaps explains the legislature's willingness to pass protective legislation for women and children, but not for men. It also explains the reluctance to place absolute limits on men's hours except where this was considered necessary to health or public safety. After 1913, however, the U.S. Supreme Court seemed willing to permit states to use their police powers to regulate hours on a very liberal interpretation of what was necessary to protect the health of even male workers. But this decision was not too effective because there was apparently little agitation for general shorter-hours legislation. The AFL opposed the legislative method before the 1930s. The New Deal hours legislation was a part of the government's total antidepression program and was therefore based mainly on "share the work" ideas. While other factors such as technological change were at work, legislation has played a role in reducing hours, especially for women and children before the 1930s and for all workers since that time. While absolute limitations on hours spread employment for all workers, standard workdays with provisions for overtime will probably increase wages for skilled workers and employment for unskilled during periods of expansion.[39] During recessions, standard workdays probably spread employment for all workers if there is unemployment among skilled workers.

Notes

1. David J. Saposs, "Colonial and Federal Beginnings," in John R. Commons, *et al., History of Labor in the United States,* New York, Macmillan Co., 1918, I, p. 160.
2. *Ibid.*
3. Cited by Helen L. Sumner, in "Part II. Citizenship (1927–1833)," in *ibid.,* p. 540.
4. *Ibid.,* pp. 540–541.
5. *Ibid.,* p. 541.
6. Cited by Elizabeth Brandeis, "Child Labor Legislation," in *ibid.,* III, 1935, p. 419.
7. *Ibid.,* p. 420.
8. *Ibid.*
9. Ritchie v. People, 155 Illinois 98 (1895).
10. Muller v. Oregon, 203 U.S. 412.
11. Holden v. Hardy, 169 U.S. 366 (1908).
12. Lochner v. New York, 198 U.S. 45.
13. Clark Kerr, John T. Dunlop, Frederick Harbison, and Charles Myers, *Industrialism and Industrial Man,* Cambridge, Harvard University Press, 1960, p. 193.
14. Helen L. Sumner, "Citizenship," *op. cit.,* p. 120.
15. *Ibid.,* p. 171.
16. Edward B. Mittelman, "Trade Unionism (1833–39)" in John R. Commons, *et al., op. cit.,* I, p. 384.
17. *Ibid.,* p. 385.
18. *Ibid.,* p. 386.
19. *Ibid.,* p. 544.
20. *Ibid.,* p. 546.
21. Ira Steward's ideas were taken over by his friend and disciple, George Gunton, who embodied them in his book *Wealth and Progress,* published in 1887. There were, however, some differences between the views of Gunton and Steward. (See Introduction to vols. IX and X of Commons, *et al., A Documentary History of American Industrial Society,* Cleveland, Arthur H. Clark Co., 1910, IX, pp. 19–51, especially fn. 4.)
22. *New York Times,* October 1, 1867, cited by Marion Cotter Cahill, *Shorter Hours,* Columbia University Studies in History, Economics and Public Law, No. 38, 1932, p. 97.
23. *Ibid.*
24. U. S. v. Martin, 94 U.S. 400.
25. Selig Perlman, *History of Trade Unionism,* New York, Augustus M. Kelly, 1950, p. 49.
26. Cahill, *op. cit.,* p. 46.
27. AFL *Convention Proceedings* (1913), p. 285; (1914), pp. 421, 443.

28. See Chap. 2.

29. 25 Statutes 57; 25 U.S. 157 (1888).

30. U. S. Department of Labor, *Growth of Labor Law in the United States,* Washington, D.C., U.S. Government Printing Office, 1962, p. 79.

31. U. S. Department of Labor, Women's Bureau, *The Effect of Labor Legislation on the Employment Opportunities for Women,* Bulletin 65, 1928.

32. Commons, *et al., op. cit.,* III, p. 540.

33. 243 U. S. 426.

34. See *American Federationist,* VL, 1934, p. 810.

35. Charles R. Roos, *NRA Economic Planning,* Cowles Commission for Research in Economics, Monograph No. 2, Bloomington, Ind., Principia Press, 1937, p. 131.

36. *Ibid.,* p. 141.

37. *Ibid.,* p. 153.

38. U. S. v. F. W. Darby Lumber Co., 312 U. S. 100.

39. See Philip W. Fleming, "The Fair Labor Standards Act in the War Economy," *Law and Contemporary Problems,* Summer 1942, p. 491; "Overtime Pay in Relation to Costs and Profits," *Monthly Labor Review,* August 1941.

4. Hours of Work in Canada

W. R. DYMOND and GEORGE SAUNDERS

Department of Labour
Ottawa, Canada

Introduction

In Canada, market forces are important in the determination of wages, hours, and other conditions of employment. There is no national uniform legislation governing conditions of work across all industry, and the legislation that has been applied to particular areas or industries has had relatively little effect on average hours worked for the economy as a whole. Such legislation is a provincial matter since most of the labor force (about 90 per cent) comes under the jurisdiction of the ten provinces. The federal government's jurisdiction extends to only 10 per cent of the Canadian labor force.

Even in the market, decisions concerning wages and working conditions are highly decentralized. There is little national or industry-wide determination of these issues. The fact of divided political jurisdiction and the regional nature of the Canadian economy, which is fostered by proximity to the United States and regional concentration of resources and output, discourage developments in these directions. For the most part, wages, hours of work, and other conditions of employment are matters settled locally at the level of the

54

individual establishment or company. The results of this system of wage setting are evident in the wide variations in both wages and hours of work that are found among establishments, industries, and areas.

It is the purpose of this chapter to describe the current structure of standard hours (normally scheduled hours of work per week as opposed to actual hours worked) of nonoffice or plant employees in Canadian industry and to note the key economic and institutional factors associated with the structure.[1]

Hours of Work Legislation in Canada

With the possible exception of early legislation affecting the hours of work of women and young persons in the latter part of the nineteenth century and first decade of the twentieth century, hours of work legislation has had little impact on the course of the standard or scheduled workweek in Canada with the exception of a few industries characterized by very long hours.[2] There is no hours legislation at present in industries under the jurisdiction of the Parliament of Canada (although such legislation is currently being introduced), and only five of the ten provinces (the four western provinces of British Columbia, Alberta, Saskatchewan and Manitoba, and Ontario) have comprehensive legislation regulating hours of work. In two of these provinces, Manitoba and Saskatchewan, limits are not imposed on hours of work but rather an overtime rate is set for hours worked beyond the maxima. In the other three provinces no work is permitted beyond the limits without permission of the administrative authority. All five provinces provide for exemptions under their acts. In general, these exemptions include seasonal industries and such industries as trucking and bus operation. The maximum hours limits under the legislation in these provinces have changed little since the 1940s.[3] A summary of this legislation is given in Table 1.

The Atlantic provinces and Quebec have no legislation similar to the other five provinces. The regulation of hours in these eastern provinces is, in the main, restricted to mining, women, and young

TABLE 1.   AVERAGE STANDARD WORKWEEK OF NONOFFICE WORKERS
(INDUSTRIAL COMPOSITE) AND PROVINCIAL HOURS LEGISLATION, 1961

(1) Province	(2) Average Standard Workweek	(3) Provincial Legislation (hours per week)
Newfoundland	48.3	No general legislation applies but specific acts or regulations impose maximum hours limits in certain lines of work, especially where women and children or hazardous occupations are involved. These limits average about 48–55 hours per week.
Prince Edward Island	45.5	
Nova Scotia	42.6	
New Brunswick	45.3	
Quebec	43.2	
Ontario	41.4	48
Manitoba	41.2	48 (44 for women)
Saskatchewan	41.2	44 (48 in smaller centers)
Alberta	41.6	44 (48 in smaller centers)
British Columbia	40.4	44

SOURCE: Column (2): See Table 2, source for Column (3); Column (3): Department of Labour, Legislation Branch, *Provincial Labour Standards,* Ottawa, December 1961.

persons. Hours regulations of a more general nature affecting individual industries and areas can be made under the industrial standards legislation of New Brunswick and Nova Scotia and the Quebec Collective Agreements Extension Act, but these regulations have had limited applicability.

Current Structure of Hours of Work

Hours of work in Canada have declined steadily since 1900 from about a level varying between 54 and 60 hours to an average level of about 42 hours (industrial composite, i.e., manufacturing and nonmanufacturing combined) in 1961.[4] Since 1944, when reliable statistics on standard hours of work were first published, the standard workweek in Canadian manufacturing shortened by about seven hours from a level of 48.2 hours. All of this reduction occurred between 1944 and 1957. There has been virtually no change in the average workweek in manufacturing since 1957.

Today (1963) 70 per cent of full-time nonoffice workers in manu-facturing work in establishments with a 40-hour workweek and 5 per cent are in establishments with less than 40 hours. In the in-dustrial composite the comparable figures are 66 and 5.[5]

Despite the achievement of a 40-hour standard workweek by the majority of Canadian nonoffice workers, longer hours of work are characteristic of groups of workers located in particular areas and industries. For example, in 1961 the workweek in the industrial composite for all of Canada averaged 42.1 hours but averaged more than this in Quebec and the Atlantic provinces (see Table 1).[6] Less than 60 per cent of the nonoffice workers canvassed in the Atlantic provinces and Quebec worked in establishments reporting a 40-hour or less standard workweek. On the other hand, more than 90 per cent of the reported nonoffice workers in British Columbia and about 70 per cent of the nonoffice workers in Ontario and the Prairies were employed in establishments with this standard.[7] On an industrial basis less than one-third of the nonoffice workers in such industries as logging, gold mining, bread products, footwear, woolen yarn, hosiery, sash, door and planing mills, wooden furniture, wooden boxes, machine shop products, auto garages, glass products, truck transportation, small hotels, laundries, and restaurants worked in establishments reporting a 40-hour or less standard workweek (see Table 2). More than 95 per cent of the workers in motor vehicles, railway rolling stock, petroleum refining and products, acids, alkalies and salts, cotton textiles, women's clothing, and primary iron and steel worked in establishments with this standard.

Three conclusions can be drawn from this brief review of hours of work in Canada. First, the 40-hour week has now been achieved by the majority of full-time nonoffice workers in most parts of Can-ada, and this goal has been reached in the absence of effective hours of work legislation. Second, very few nonoffice workers have a work-week of less than 40 hours. According to 1963 figures, most of these workers are in clothing, printing and publishing, and retail trade.[8] Third, the 40-hour standard has not penetrated to any great extent

TABLE 2. NONOFFICE EMPLOYMENT, HOURS OF WORK, WAGES, VALUE-ADDED PER MAN-HOUR
RATIO OF WAGE PAYROLL TO VALUE-ADDED AND EXTENT OF
COLLECTIVE BARGAINING, BY INDUSTRY

Industry	(1) Nonoffice Employees	(2) Average Standard Hours	(3) Nonoffice Employment by Standard Hours Intervals			(4) Average Hours Paid For	(5) Average Hourly Earnings	(6) Value-Added Per Man-Hour	(7) Ratio of Wage Payroll to Value-Added	(8) Workers Under Collective Agreement
			40 and Under	Over 40 to 45	Over 45					
			%	%	%		$	$	%	%
Logging	52,579	50.2	15	19	66	–	–	–	–	88
Gold mining	12,955	44.1	3	92	5	42.7	1.72	–	–	59
Iron mining	6,379	41.8	80		20	45.2	2.48	–	–	93
Metal mining (other than gold & iron)	27,102	41.0	79	17	4	42.0[a]	2.39[a]	–	–	93
Coal mining	8,862	40.4	94	6		39.7	1.77	–	–	89
Manufacturing	845,317	41.5	71	20	9	40.6	1.83	5.0	49.2	65
Slaughtering & meat packing	18,984	41.1	77	18	5	40.4	1.89	4.6	52.1	85
Dairy products	19,840	42.1	72	10	18	–	–	–	56.7	64
Canned & cured fish	12,256	47.3	34	9	57	34.9	1.15	2.9	51.0	54
Flour mills	2,918	40.5	91	5	4	42.2[b]	1.77[b]	8.0	32.6	81
Biscuits	5,710	41.5	66	24	10	39.2	1.37	3.9	39.8	59
Bread & other bakery products	18,558	42.7	31	46	23	41.9	1.48	2.7	62.0	46
Carbonated beverages	6,934	43.3	47	27	26	–	–	–	25.1	10
Breweries	6,726	40.1	98	2		39.7	2.34	14.0	22.0	97
Confectionery	7,122	41.7	47	50	3	40.0	1.30	3.7	42.9	42
Tobacco, cigars & cigarettes	6,289	40.2	96	4		39.6	1.83	6.3	32.7	93
Rubber products	13,362	41.8	59	35	6	41.3	1.87	5.6	46.2	86
Rubber footwear	4,077	44.7	–	88	12	41.7	1.39	–	–	81

Product										
products (nes)	9,285	40.6	85	11	4	41.1	2.05	–	–	88
Boots & shoes	13,456	44.3	18	60	22	40.2	1.18	2.2	64.2	36
Leather tanneries & other leather products	6,753	42.5	51	45	4	40.9	1.36	2.8	62.9	45
Cotton yarn & cloth	13,827	40.2	96	4	–	40.4	1.40	2.7	61.9	89
Woolen yarn & cloth	7,387	44.2	30	47	23	43.1	1.29	2.5	56.3	71
Synthetic & silk textiles	10,782	43.8	35	40	25	43.3	1.45	4.4	49.9	68
Men's & boys' suits & overcoats	9,401	40.0	99	1	–	} 37.7	} 1.18	–	–	80
Men's fine shirts	5,029	41.4	53	47	–			–	–	57
Work clothing & sportswear	7,456	40.8	82	18	–	–	–	–	–	51
Women's & misses' coats & suits	3,037	37.7	99	–	1	} 36.8	} 1.25	–	–	70
Women's & misses' dresses	4,850	40.0	98	2	–			–	–	69
Hosiery & other knitted goods	13,830	43.7	29	56	15	40.8	1.10	2.3	57.5	34
Foundation garments	2,749	40.8	55	44	1	–	–	–	49.1	40
Fur goods	1,648	39.2	86	13	1	–	–	–	60.9	60
Plywood & veneer mills	7,535	42.3	65	21	14	40.1	1.70	3.1	59.3	78
Sash, door & planing mills	12,030	45.3	27	36	37	42.0	1.44	3.1	58.8	44
Sawmills	26,028	43.8	62	12	26	39.8	1.85	3.5	58.2	62
Wooden furniture	13,526	44.1	28	45	27	42.4	1.47	2.9	63.6	40
Wooden boxes, baskets & misc. wood products	1,390	43.5	40	45	15	42.1	1.34	2.9	60.5	41
Paper boxes & cartons	9,596	40.5	73	27	–	40.8	1.67	4.0	52.3	81
Pulp & paper	52,837	40.3	95	2	3	41.3	2.34	6.7	42.4	95
Newsprint	37,792	40.1	99	–	1	–	–	–	–	95
Paper other than newsprint	4,976	40.9	81	12	7	–	–	–	–	97
Pulp	10,069	40.6	89	3	8	–	–	–	–	96
Printing, publishing & allied industries	35,410	38.8	92	7	1	38.9	2.22	6.4	55.8	55
Daily newspapers	9,868	38.8	91	6	3	–	–	–	–	71
Printing & pub. other than newspapers	25,542	38.8	92	8	–	–	–	–	–	48

a Other metal mining, including iron mining.
b Grain mill products.

TABLE 2 (Continued)

Industry	(1) Nonoffice Employees	(2) Average Standard Hours	(3) Nonoffice Employment by Standard Hours Intervals			(4) Average Hours Paid For	(5) Average Hourly Earnings	(6) Value-Added Per Man-Hour	(7) Ratio of Wage Payroll to Value-Added	(8) Workers Under Collective Agreement
			40 and Under	Over 40 to 45	Over 45					
			%	%	%		$	$	%	%
Agricultural implements	7,767	40.4	92	7	1	39.5	2.16	3.5	79.1	79
Heating & cooking apparatus	5,685	40.8	84	10	6	40.5	1.80	5.1	50.8	81
Household, office & store machinery	5,558	40.8	71	28	1	40.6	2.01	5.4	51.1	61
Iron castings	8,895	40.9	77	20	3	41.3	2.01	4.2	57.9	69
Machine shop products	3,671	43.0	39	50	11	–	–	–	64.5	32
Machine tools	2,368	41.2	66	30	4	–	–	–	80.8	63
Industrial machinery	14,969	41.3	70	25	5	41.3	1.98	5.7	53.7	64
Primary iron & steel	28,425	40.0	100	–	–	40.2	2.54	6.3	46.4	74
Sheet metal products	7,815	40.8	80	18	2	41.5	2.08	5.3	52.9	76
Aircraft & parts	18,753	40.2	95	5	–	41.8	2.11	4.7	72.7	84
Auto repair & garages	1,600	46.7	7	33	60	–	–	–	–	5
Motor vehicles	21,833	40.2	96	3	1	41.3	2.34	7.6	41.5	98
Motor vehicle parts & accessories	12,896	40.6	84	14	2	40.1	2.09	4.7	56.2	85
Railway rolling stock	2,591	40.0	100	–	–	39.5	2.03	2.8	84.1	89
Shipbuilding & repairing	11,617	40.3	83	17	–	39.2	2.04	3.4	68.5	89
Brass & copper products	3,823	40.7	79	20	1	41.0	2.00	4.9	52.2	68
Heavy electrical machinery & equipment	9,646	40.2	90	10	–	40.8	2.08	6.5	56.8	76
Refrigerators, vacuum cleaners, etc.	19,079	40.5	85	15	–	39.6	1.91	5.5	46.1	66

Radio, television & other elec. equipment	10,926	40.5	87	13	–	40.5	1.74	4.9	66.2	64
Clay products	3,094	43.6	33	53	14	42.2	1.69	4.2	48.5	68
Petroleum refining & products	7,731	40.2	96	4	–	41.2	2.60	14.5	33.3	48
Acids, alkalies & salts	4,359	40.1	98	2	–	40.7	2.36	9.2	37.6	94
Medicinal, pharm. & toilet preparations	6,577	39.8	90	7	3	40.0	1.56	11.7	25.9	14
Paints, varnishes & lacquers	2,851	40.2	93	7	–	40.5	1.88	10.0	35.5	70
Misc. manufacturing industries	22,965	42.0	55	34	11	41.4	1.50	4.2	53.4	38
Urban & suburban transportation	16,154	40.9	68	30	2	–	2.11	–	–	95
Truck transport	20,812	48.8	15	19	66	–	1.73	–	–	65
Grain elevators	3,119	40.8	84	14	2	–	–	–	–	59
Electrical light & power	27,708	40.4	87	12	1	–	–	–	–	70
Wholesale trade	46,138	42.7	53	28	19	–	–	–	–	21
Retail trade (grocery, meat, & dept. stores)	23,712	42.0	50	42	8	–	–	–	–	43
Retail trade (ex. grocery, meat, & dept. stores)	110,375	41.5	67	20	13	–	–	–	–	7
Hotels (200 or more employees, ex. railways)	4,520	42.9	52	25	23	⎫	⎫	–	–	69
Hotels (less than 200 employees, ex. railways)	12,908	45.0	24	30	46	⎬ 38.7	⎬ 1.04	–	–	28
Railway hotels	5,997	40.1	99	–	1	⎪	⎪	–	–	97
Restaurants	19,094	45.6	22	27	51	⎭	⎭	–	–	8
Laundries & dry cleaning	15,091	43.6	31	49	20	39.7	1.03	–	–	25
Industrial composite	1,265,210	42.1	65	21	14	–	–	–	–	57

SOURCES: *Columns 1 and 3*, Department of Labour, Economics and Research Branch, *Special Tabulation* from October 1961 annual survey of Wage Rates, Salaries and Hours of Labour; *Column 2, ibid.*, and Department of Labour, Economics and Research Branch, *Wage Rates, Salaries and Hours of Labour, Report No. 44*, October 1961, Ottawa, Table 88; *Column 8*, Department of Labour, Economics and Research Branch, *Special Tabulation* from May 1961 annual survey of Working Conditions; *Columns 4 and 5*, Dominion Bureau of Statistics, *Manhours and Hourly Earnings*, Ottawa, 1961; *Column 6*, Dominion Bureau of Statistics, *General Review of the Manufacturing Industries*, Ottawa, 1959 and *Manhours and Hourly Earnings*, Ottawa, 1959; *Column 7*, Dominion Bureau of Statistics, *General Review of the Manufacturing Industries*, Ottawa, 1959.

into certain geographical and industrial sectors of the Canadian economy. In these sectors the workweek remains above 40 hours for significant numbers of nonoffice workers.

Economic and Institutional Analysis of the Structure of Hours of Work in Canada[9]

Productivity

Perhaps the most important economic factor affecting conditions of work is productivity. Historically, workers have taken their share of productivity gains in the form of higher wages, better working conditions, or shorter hours. When taken in the form of shorter hours, their hourly wages are usually raised in order to maintain take-home pay. It would be expected, therefore, that productivity, hourly wages, and shorter hours would be related. The facts appear to support this expectation (see Table 2). Since there are no adequate measures of productivity in Canada, value-added data have been used and are related to man-hours to obtain a rough measure of the level of productivity in various manufacturing industries.[10]

The average value-added per man-hour in industries with average standard hours of less than 42.1 (the average for the industrial composite) is twice that of industries with average standard hours of 42.1 or longer. For the same two groups of industries, average hourly earnings in the "short" hours group are 36 per cent higher than average hourly earnings in the "long" hours group.[11]

A rank correlation of value-added per man-hour and standard hours by industry gives a value of −.54. Similarly, a rank correlation of average hourly earnings and standard hours by industry gives a value of −.53. Although these correlations are significant at the 5 per cent level, their relatively low values reflect the phenomenon of growing numbers of Canadian plant workers achieving the 40-hour workweek but few of them taking their increased leisure in the form of workweeks below 40. In recent years there has been a trend to more holidays and other time off.[12] If it had been possible to calculate the contribution of these holidays and time-off practices to the standard workweek, the correlation coefficients might very well have been higher.

Size of Establishment and Concentration

A close relation exists between size of establishment and the length of the standard workweek (see Table 3). The standard workweek is almost three hours shorter on the average in establishments with 1,000 or more employees than in establishments with 15 to 24 employees. Ninety per cent of plant employees in establishments with more than 1,000 employees are in plants reporting 40 hours per week or less; less than 50 per cent of the workers in plants employing less than 50 employees are in establishments with similar short hours. About half of the employees in small plants (less than 50 employees) are in establishments that work 44 hours or more, whereas only 7 per cent of the employees in the very large establishments (1,000 or more employees) are in plants reporting these hours. A similar relation between size of establishment and hours of work occurs within different industries including mining, manu-

TABLE 3. AVERAGE STANDARD HOURS OF WORK
OF NONOFFICE EMPLOYEES, INDUSTRIAL COMPOSITE,
BY SIZE OF ESTABLISHMENT, 1962

Size of Establishment (Number of employees)	Average Standard Hours
1,000 and over	40.5
500 – 999	40.9
200 – 499	41.7
100 – 199	42.2
50 – 99	42.7
25 – 49	43.1
15 – 24	43.3

SOURCE: Department of Labour, Economics and Research Branch, *Special Tabulation* from October 1962 annual survey of Wage Rates, Salaries and Hours of Labour, Ottawa.

facturing, transportation, storage, communications and public utilities, trade, and service.

It is not clear from the statistics, however, whether these conditions reflect genuine economies of scale (productivity) or protected product markets which enable large establishments to pass on rising costs to the consumer. Elements of both are undoubtedly present. Large establishments tend to be more efficient than small establishments. On the other hand, in a country in which product markets are widely dispersed geographically, individual large establishments may exercise some monopoly power in local markets.[13]

Labor Intensity

Where a high proportion of the value of the product goes to labor, employers are in a less favorable position to grant preferred conditions of work than employers whose labor costs are a small proportion of total costs. A rank correlation between the degree of labor intensity as measured by the ratio of total wages to value-added and the length of the workweek gives a value of only .23 which is not significant at the 5 per cent level. This correlation is not inconsistent with the higher correlations found between productivity and hours. A number of industries with higher than average "labor intensity" are also industries with higher than average productivity. Most of these industries are in the printing and publishing, iron and steel, and electrical supplies groups, and virtually all enjoy, on the average, 40 or near 40-hour workweeks (see Table 2).

Regional Influences

Marked economic and social differences among Canada's regions exercise an important influence on the structure of hours of work. The Atlantic region is Canada's least developed region.[14] It is isolated from markets in central Canada and the United States and is characterized by a predominantly unskilled, relatively weakly unionized labor force and high rates of unemployment. At the other extreme, British Columbia, on Canada's West Coast, is an advanced economic area based on its proximity to the rich markets of the Pacific North-west, an abundance of natural resources, and a highly skilled, highly unionized labor force. The remaining three regions, Quebec, Ontario, and the Prairie provinces, lie between these two extremes. Ontario, which is the center of Canada's manufacturing and service industry, enjoys a level of living approximating that of British Columbia. Quebec, also a large manufacturing and mining area, is developing rapidly but still lags behind its neighbor Ontario. The Prairie prov-inces, based on mechanized wheat farming, oil, and gas, are also enjoying a very rapid economic development.

Scheduled hours of work conform closely to these regional eco-nomic differences. The standard workweek is longest in the Atlantic region and shortest in British Columbia. In general, the standard workweek shortens as one moves from east to west reaching an average level of 40.4 hours on the West Coast (see Table 1 on p. 56). A similar dispersion of hours of work is indicated by a comparison of scheduled workweeks among metropolitan areas representing the different regions and by a comparison of individual industries by province (see Table 4).[15]

The regional structure of hours of work by industry (Table 4) shows very wide variations. In some industries such as canning, bakery products, sawmills, auto garages, and small hotels, the varia-tion from one province to another is about nine hours or more. These industries are generally low productivity, relatively poorly unionized, and usually employ a labor force that is predominantly unskilled. Conditions of work in such industries are heavily influenced by local conditions and therefore closely reflect regional economic patterns. On the other hand, a number of other industries that are located in the various provinces show much less regional dispersion in hours. These include the meatpacking, breweries, pulp and paper, primary iron and steel, and printing and publishing industries, which are generally highly unionized, have relatively high levels of productivity, serve national markets, and employ a relatively skilled labor force. Working conditions in these industries are less subject to local in-

TABLE 4. AVERAGE STANDARD HOURS OF WORK AND PER CENT UNDER COLLECTIVE AGREEMENTS IN SELECTED INDUSTRIES, BY PROVINCE, 1961[a]

H = Average Standard Hours.
U = Per Cent Under Collective Agreements.

Industry	Canada		Newfoundland		Nova Scotia		New Brunswick		Quebec	
	H	U	H	U	H	U	H	U	H	U
Manufacturing	41.5	67	45.0	72	43.1	69	44.2	57	42.2	64
Slaughtering and meat packing	41.1	85	–	–	–	–	41.6	85[b]	41.4	80
Dairy products	42.1	64	–	–	42.9	45	45.4	–	46.2	52
Canned and cured fish	47.3	54	52.2	53	46.7	70	52.1	5	57.7	[b]
Bread and other bakery products	42.7	46	43.9	75	46.5	51	47.7	40	44.7	29
Flour mills	40.5	81	–	–	–	–	–	–	40.3	94
Breweries	40.1	97	45.0	67	40.0	83	40.0	100	40.0	98
Hosiery and other knitted goods	43.7	34	–	–	41.2	30	46.7	[b]	44.6	33
Sawmills	43.8	62	–	–	52.0	[b]	53.1	19	53.5	35
Sash, door and planing mills	45.3	44	49.7	41	44.3	20	46.8	57	49.8	33
Wooden furniture	44.1	40	–	–	46.8	[b]	–	–	46.3	36
Pulp and paper	40.3	95	40.0	94	42.2	100	40.3	97	40.4	97
Printing and publishing	38.8	56	41.2	70	39.2	55	39.3	53	39.0	53
Iron castings	40.9	69	–	–	40.0	100	41.4	77	41.4	77
Primary iron and steel	40.0	74	–	–	40.0	100	–	–	40.0	98
Auto repair and garages	46.7	45	–	–	40.0	86	–	–	49.8	[b]
Clay products	43.6	68	–	–	40.0	99	–	–	44.8	68
Truck transport	48.8	65	43.9	[b]	47.9	33	50.7	13	50.5	57
Hotels (less than 200 employees)	45.0	28	48.0	[b]	47.6	69[b]	47.3	[b]	49.0	[b]
Restaurants	45.6	8	43.8	[b]	48.0	[b]	47.4	[b]	48.8	6

Industry	Ontario		Manitoba		Saskatchewan		Alberta		British Columbia	
	H	U	H	U	H	U	H	U	H	U
Manufacturing	41.1	68	41.0	59	40.7	67	41.2	68	40.3	84
Slaughtering and meat packing	42.0	78	40.2	97	40.0	92	40.1	94	40.0	96
Dairy products	41.2	66	41.3	69	40.3	72	40.5	75	40.1	91
Canned and cured fish	47.6	11	–	–	–	–	–	–	40.0	90
Bread and other bakery products	42.8	48	38.8	73	38.2	77	38.8	57	36.6	77
Flour mills	41.3	70	40.3	76	40.0	96	40.1	75	–	–
Breweries	40.1	98	40.0	94	40.0	98	40.0	99	40.0	100
Hosiery and other knitted goods	43.3	38	–	–	–	b	–	–	–	–
Sawmills	48.2	33	–	–	50.5	b	47.4	11	40.5	78
Sash, door and planing mills	44.5	35	44.0	30	42.4	50	44.9	9	41.1	74
Wooden furniture	42.7	46	43.4	11	–	–	42.4	10	40.5	45
Pulp and paper	40.1	98	–	–	–	–	–	–	40.0	98
Printing and publishing	38.5	54	40.7	35	39.4	49	40.9	70	37.9	78
Iron castings	40.8	69	40.3	40	40.0	13	40.3	25	40.0	69
Primary iron and steel	40.0	69	–	–	–	–	–	–	–	b
Auto repair and garages	46.4	b	47.3	23	45.4	b	43.9	b	40.5	b
Clay products	44.3	56	43.5	36	40.0	100	42.7	100	40.0	89
Truck transport	47.0	78	49.3	49	44.8	43	44.0	37	41.6	78
Hotels (less than 200 employees)	45.4	36	45.1	7	44.0	4	43.3	27	40.6	53
Restaurants	45.4	6	42.1	3	44.2	7	43.3	2	41.3	31

SOURCE: See Table 2, sources for columns 2 and 8.

a Prince Edward Island not included because of insufficient information.

b Less than 1 per cent.

fluences. In British Columbia nearly all industries are at 40 or close to a 40-hour workweek on the average.[16] In the Atlantic provinces, at the other extreme, only a few industries, the highly unionized and highly productive industries, enjoy similar workweeks.

Another dimension of the regional structure of hours of work is the difference in the standard workweek by size of urban area. For communities in population size categories above 10,000, little difference exists in standard hours of work. In smaller communities (below 10,000 population) hours of work are longer (see Table 5). Only 55 per cent of the nonoffice workers in small areas (less than

TABLE 5. AVERAGE STANDARD HOURS OF WORK OF
NONOFFICE EMPLOYEES, INDUSTRIAL COMPOSITE,
BY SIZE OF URBAN AREA, 1962

Size of Urban Area (population)	Average Standard Hours
500,000 and over	41.3
100,000 – 499,999	41.1
50,000 – 99,999	41.4
25,000 – 49,999	41.3
10,000 – 24,999	41.6
Under 10,000	42.9

SOURCE: Department of Labour, Economics and Research Branch, *Special Tabulation* from October 1962 annual survey of Wage Rates, Salaries and Hours of Labour, Ottawa.

10,000 population) are in establishments with a standard workweek of 40 hours or less and 23 per cent are employed in establishments that work 48 hours or longer. In urban areas larger than 10,000, about 70 to 75 per cent of nonoffice employees work in establishments that schedule 40 or less hours per week; less than 10 per cent are in establishments with 48 hours or more. The larger urban areas enjoy greater economic activity, more active and competitive labor markets, and greater union activity than smaller urban areas which are dependent on servicing the surrounding agricultural areas.

Unionism and Hours

The degree of unionism and shorter hours show a relatively close correlation. On an interindustry basis a rank correlation between standard hours of work and extent of collective bargaining gives a value of —.46 which is significant at the 5 per cent level.[17] Unionism is also correlated with productivity. The coefficient of rank correlation between productivity and the extent of collective bargaining is .37, significant at the 5 per cent level.[18] The relation between unionism, hours, and productivity is also reflected in the tendency for unions to be concentrated in larger establishments.[19] As already noted, such establishments, which may be more efficient than smaller establishments, enjoy shorter standard workweeks. However, to the extent that large establishments signify oligopoly or monopoly positions, the relation between unionism and size of establishment may also reflect the tendency for unions to be found in concentrated industries.[20]

Within the different provinces, British Columbia enjoys a 40 or near 40-hour workweek in nearly all of the industries surveyed regardless of degree of unionization (see Table 4). In the remaining provinces, the highly unionized industries tend to have shorter hours than the less unionized industries. For the most part, these unionized industries also enjoy high levels of productivity or employ a relatively highly skilled labor force. However, there are examples of highly organized but relatively low productivity industries enjoying 40 or near 40-hour workweeks. As already indicated, most of these industries are found in British Columbia but some are also found in other provinces. For example, in this category are clothing, cotton textiles, shipbuilding, and railway rolling stock which are located mainly in the eastern provinces. These industries are found predominantly in or near large urban areas where shorter hours are an important condition of work, or are oligopolistic in nature.[21]

On the other hand, there are important examples of highly organized but low productivity industries or sectors of industries which have "long" workweeks. These include industries located in the eastern provinces such as truck transport, canning, and the unionized sector of service. Longer hours in these industries reflect their special characteristics and their geographic location.

On the whole, unionism is associated with the shorter workweek, but this relation appears to be tied to the association between unionism and productivity, concentration, or geographic location.

Summary and Conclusions

Despite the absence of effective legislation, the 40-hour week is now the standard for the majority of full-time nonoffice workers in Canada. Longer workweeks are still in effect for concentrations of workers in particular industries and areas.

An analysis of the structure of the workweek reveals that productivity or "ability to pay," geographic location, and unionism are the key factors separating those nonoffice workers now on a 40-hour or close to 40-hour workweek and those working longer hours. In general, nonoffice workers employed in unionized industries with relatively high productivity or protected product markets work a shorter standard workweek than other nonoffice workers. Also, hours of work in large urban areas and in Ontario and the western provinces tend to be shorter than in smaller urban areas and in the provinces of Quebec and the Atlantic region. In British Columbia nearly all of the nonoffice workers surveyed enjoy 40 or near 40-hour workweeks. British Columbia is a high wage, high productivity, highly unionized area where labor market competition is sufficiently active to ensure the adoption of preferred conditions of employment across most of the province. Wage levels in Canada have been found to be affected in a similar way.[22]

It was not possible statistically to determine how productivity or ability to pay, unionism, and labor market activity are each related to hours of work. However, a possible causal relation among these factors may be offered to help explain their individual relation to the development of shorter hours of work. Reductions in the workweek with the same take-home pay are only possible where industry is productive and can afford to pay high hourly wages to ensure no loss in pay when hours are reduced. In many of the very long hours situations such reductions themselves may produce offsetting increases in productivity and therefore are costless to industry. But beyond a certain level continued reductions in hours add to costs.[23] In these cases, productivity advances (or product market concentration) become a necessary condition for further reductions, but by themselves may not ensure shorter hours. It is in these instances that union activity and an active and competitive labor market might have played an important role in bringing hours down to 40 or less for the majority of Canadian workers. Collective bargaining serves to articulate workers' preference for more leisure. An active and competitive labor market helps to ensure the widespread adoption of this preference. The uniformly shorter hours of work in British Columbia and the variations in hours of work by productivity, product market concentration, and unionism in the remainder of the country are in line with this explanation.

Finally, it has been noticed that in the prosperous, advanced sectors of the economy, where most full-time nonoffice workers enjoy a 40-hour workweek, few of these workers work shorter hours. This phenomenon reflects the choice of workers who work a standard workweek of 40 hours to take their leisure in other forms. In recent years, holidays and other time paid for but not worked have been increasing. This trend suggests that the issue of the shorter workweek (that is, workweeks below 40 hours), which is currently receiving so much attention, is not only one of whether industry can afford it, but is to a greater extent one of workers choosing alternative means of reducing their worktime.

Notes

1. Office employees are not included in the study in this article because of lack of space. However, it is worthy of note that the overwhelming majority of these employees enjoy fairly uniform standard hours across the country.

According to a Canadian Department of Labour survey in 1963, about 94 per cent of office workers in Canada were employed in establishments reporting a scheduled workweek for these employees ranging between 35 and 40 hours. This record is in contrast to the longer and more variable standard hours of nonoffice workers. See page 57 of text and fn. 5.

2. For a history of hours of work legislation in Canada see Edith Lorentsen and Evelyn Woolner, "Fifty Years of Labour Legislation in Canada," *Labour Gazette,* Ottawa, Canada, September 1950; Department of Labour, *Legislation Branch, Labour Legislation of the Past Decade,* Ottawa 1963; and *Provincial Labour Standards,* annual, Ottawa.

3. Lorentsen and Woolner, *op. cit.,* p. 1453 and *Labour Legislation of the Past Decade,* pp. 11, 12.

4. H. D. Woods and Sylvia Ostry, *Labour Policy and Labour Economics in Canada,* Toronto, 1962, p. 335; Department of Labour, *Wages and Hours of Labour in Canada* (now called Wage Rates, Salaries and Hours of Labour), annual, Ottawa, various issues; and Table 2 in this chapter.

5. Department of Labour, Economics and Research Branch, *Working Conditions in Canadian Industry,* annual, Ottawa, 1963, pp. 6, 10 (hereafter called *Working Conditions Report*).

6. These figures are from a special tabulation made in the Economics and Research Branch of the Canadian Department of Labour and on which the remainder of this study is based.

7. Throughout the study reference is made to statistical materials which could not be published in this article because of lack of space. These include distributions of nonoffice employees by standard hours by province, size of establishment, metropolitan area, size of urban area, and union status.

8. *Working Conditions Report, 1963,* pp. 6–21.

9. For recent examples of cross-sectional studies of hours of work in the United States see T. Aldrich Finegan, "Hours of Work in the United States: A Cross-Sectional Analysis," *Journal of Political Economy,* October 1962; and *Monthly Labor Review,* "Hours of Work in the United States and Abroad," Washington, August 1963.

10. There are, as yet, no official man-hour statistics available in Canada. To obtain a measure of man-hours for this study, average hourly earnings were divided into wage payroll statistics (see Note on Statistical Sources at the end of this section).

11. Both manufacturing and nonmanufacturing industries are included in the average hourly earnings calculations whereas only manufacturing industries are included in the value-added per man-hour calculations (see Note on Statistical Sources at the end of this section). Almost the same results were obtained using the same industries for the calculations of average hourly earnings and value-added per man-hour.

12. This trend can be seen from an examination of the Department of Labour surveys of working conditions. See, for example, *Working Conditions Reports,* 1957 to 1963. In the United States it has been estimated that paid vacation and holiday time is now equivalent to about two hours per week, which represents an increase of 20 per cent since 1948. See Sar A. Levitan, *Reducing Worktime as a Means to Combat Unemployment,* The W. E. Upjohn Institute for Employment Research, 1964, p. 7.

13. There are no currently available measures of concentration in Canada. The latest such measures relate to the year 1948 and are limited to manufacturing industries only. See Gideon Rosenbluth, *Concentration in Canadian Manufacturing Industries*, National Bureau of Economic Research, Princeton, 1957. It was possible to match twenty-eight of Professor Rosenbluth's industries to the industries in Table 2 of this chapter. A rank correlation between average standard hours and concentration (as measured by the number of firms accounting for 80 per cent of employment) in these twenty-eight industries gives a value of .54 significant at the 5 per cent level. Also see The Canadian Bank of Commerce, *Industrial Concentration*, Royal Commission on Canada's Economic Prospects, Ottawa, June 1956; and H. Edward English, *Industrial Structure in Canada's International Competitive Position*, The Private Planning Association of Canada, Montreal, 1964, for recent discussions of the relation between firm size and the product market in Canada.

14. For a regional analysis of the Canadian economy see R. D. Howland, *Some Regional Aspects of Canada's Economic Development*, Royal Commission on Canada's Economic Prospects, Ottawa, 1957.

15. See fn. 7.

16. See Table 4 in this chapter and also Department of Labour, Economics and Research Branch, *Wage Rates, Salaries and Hours of Labour*, Report No. 44, October 1961, Ottawa, Table 88, for more examples.

17. The correlation is subject to the same considerations affecting the correlation between productivity and wages and hours (see p. 62).

18. The correlation between unionism and standard hours of work is based on both manufacturing and nonmanufacturing industries and therefore includes a larger number of industries than that used for the correlation between unionism and productivity. A higher correlation, $-.515$, is obtained between unionism and hours in the sample of industries used for the unionism and productivity correlation.

19. It was not possible to develop a tabulation from these statistics showing the relation between establishment size, hours of work, and extent of collective bargaining. However, in a special tabulation of employers' returns from the 1955 annual survey of working conditions in Canada, a close relation was found between establishment size and unionization. Almost 90 per cent of establishments with 1,000 or more employees and more than four-fifths of establishments with 500 to 999 employees reported unions covering 50 per cent or more of their nonoffice employees. The comparable percentages for establishments with 15 to 24 employees and 25 to 49 employees are 26 and 35.

20. Using Professor Rosenbluth's measure of concentration, a rank correlation between extent of collective bargaining and concentration for the twenty-eight industries for which data are available gives a value of .63.

21. According to Professor Rosenbluth's measures, in 1948, cotton textiles had a concentration ratio of 5.1 (number of firms accounting for 80 per cent of employment); shipbuilding, a ratio of 13.1; and railway rolling stock, a ratio of 3.1, all indicating high concentration relative to the concentration ratios of other industries in Rosenbluth's sample. See Rosenbluth, *op. cit.*, Table A–1.

22. See Woods and Ostry, *op. cit.*, chaps. XV, XVI, XVII; and George

Saunders, *Wage Determination in Canada,* Department of Labour, Economics and Research Branch, January 1964, mimeographed.

23. Reynolds suggests that this level lies between 40 and 50 hours for most occupations. Denison places the level at 48.6, the average normal workweek in the United States in 1929. See L. G. Reynolds, *Labor Economics and Labor Relations,* New York, Prentice-Hall, 1959, and Edward F. Denison, *The Sources of Economic Growth in the United States,* Supplementary Paper No. 13, Committee for Economic Development, 1962, p. 40.

Note on Statistical Sources

Standard hours statistics for the analysis on pp. 62–70 were taken from the Department of Labour, Economics and Research Branch, *Wage Rates, Salaries and Hours of Labour,* Report No. 44, October 1961, Ottawa, Table 88, and from special tabulations of the information collected in the October 1961 and 1962 surveys of wage rates, salaries, and hours of labor. The data from the October 1961 survey provided statistics on standard hours by industry and by industry within province. The October 1962 survey provided information on standard hours by size of establishment and size of urban area. Information on extent of collective bargaining (as measured by the per cent of workers covered by a collective agreement—these statistics are reported by employers on an establishment basis) was taken from a special tabulation of employers' returns to the Department of Labour's annual survey of working conditions in Canada, May 1961. Both the wage rates and working conditions surveys cover substantially the same establishments. In most industries these include all establishments with fifteen or more employees; in some industries smaller establishments are also included. The industrial coverage of the study corresponds to that in *Wage Rates, Salaries and Hours of Labour,* Report No. 44, except for industries where information from other sources necessary to perform the analysis was not available. Standard hours for manufacturing as a whole and for the industrial composite include all observations. Major industries excluded from the analysis are agriculture, fishing, construction, water, air and railway transportation, communications, finance, insurance and real estate, and government service.

Data on average hourly earnings and average hours paid for come from Dominion Bureau of Statistics monthly surveys of man-hours and hourly earnings. These surveys usually cover establishments with fifteen or more employees and the results are published on the same standard industrial classification as those of the Department of Labour, therefore facilitating comparisons of the statistics of the two agencies.

Statistics on value-added and payrolls, which were used to develop measures of productivity and labor intensity, come from Dominion Bureau of Statistics, *General Review of the Manufacturing Industries,* 1959. This publication is based on surveys of all manufacturing establishments. Because the General Review has been published on a new standard industrial classification since 1960, the value-added and payroll statistics and, consequently, the measures of productivity and labor intensity relate to the year 1959. Since reliable or consistent statistics on value-added in the nonmanufacturing industries could not be obtained, productivity and labor intensity measures were not developed for the individual industries in that sector.

The following table shows the number of industries used in the rank correlation analysis. The data for the analysis (except concentration) are included in Table 2.

NUMBER OF INDUSTRIES USED IN THE RANK CORRELATION ANALYSIS

Variables Correlated	Number of Industries
Value-added per man-hour and standard hours	45
Average hourly earnings and standard hours	52
Ratio of wage payroll to value-added and standard hours	51
Concentration and standard hours	28
Unionism and standard hours	78
Unionism and productivity	45
Unionism and concentration	28

NOTE: Industry groups were not used in the correlations if information for subindustries was available.

5. Hours of Work and Moonlighting*

PAUL E. MOTT

Department of Sociology
Wharton School of Finance and Commerce
University of Pennsylvania

The sociology of work has long been concerned with the impact of a person's job on his behavior in nonjob situations. The basic hypothesis in this field—that various aspects of the job affect the worker's attitudes, behavior, mental health, style of life, and so on— is still dominant. Such organizational characteristics as "mass" versus "bureaucratic" industrial structures, orderliness of career patterns, the extent of repetitiousness in work, and styles of supervision are examples of the causal factors currently being studied.

One aspect of the work situation that can have great effects on the worker is the span of hours during which he works at his primary job. There are various characteristics of the span of working hours that are relevant for studying his behavior, attitudes, and health. The span of working hours can vary in average length each day. The hours of work may be continuous or split into smaller blocks of time. They may blend almost indistinguishably with free time or be quite distinct from it. The hours of work may occur during different

* The research for this chapter was conducted under a grant (M–3276) from the National Institutes of Health, U.S. Public Health Service, Bethesda, Maryland.

parts of the 24-hour day; in other words, the person may be on shift work. But even among shift workers the span of hours worked may change periodically; they may work the day shift one week, the afternoon shift the next week, the night shift the following week, and begin the cycle again during the weeks that follow. Each of these variations in the span of hours during which the person works can affect his nonjob life.[1] In this chapter I am concerned primarily about one aspect of this span-of-hours concept: the effects of the number of hours each day or week during which the person works at his primary job.

Earlier in the volume it was shown that the length of the workday or workweek is decreasing for many categories of workers, particularly factory workers. The trend has not escaped the attention of sociologists, but their investigations have focused primarily on the uses to which the workers put their leisure rather than their free time. The difference between the concepts of leisure and free time is crucial for what gets studied as well as what does not. Free time is the span of hours available to the person each day after subtracting his time at work, preparing for work (grooming, transportation), and time for tending to the needs of his organism (eating, sleeping).[2] The concept of leisure time implies a state or quality of free time: that it is used for nonwork. While the concept of leisure time is commonly used synonymously with free time, it can be misleading to do so. It can lead the investigator away from the possibility that the person will use some of his free time at a second job.

One of the earliest suggestions of this application of free time was made by Harvey Swados in his study of the uses of free time in Akron, Ohio.[3] Swados selected Akron for two reasons. First, the workers in the rubber industry there were on a six-hour workday. Second, the community was relatively devoid of organized opportunities for leisure activity. Swados found that a large proportion of the rubber industry workers were using their free time to work at second jobs. The convergence of these two conditions—the decreasing amount of worktime and limited facilities for the pursuit of leisure activities—had created a situation favorable to taking second jobs.

Similarly, as the national workweek has shortened, the incidence of moonlighting has increased. The number of known moonlighters has increased from 1.8 million in 1952 to 3.3 million in 1962.[4] This last figure represents 5 per cent of all employed workers.

The incidence of moonlighting is highest among farm, construction, educational services, entertainment, recreation, and public employees. Two-fifths of the moonlighters are likely to be self-employed on their second job, which gives them some control over the hours that they work at that job. Most of the remaining workers are in the trade or service industries. The most common pattern is for the worker to take a second job in the same occupational category as his first job; common examples are the television repairmen who work for someone else at their primary job and repair sets privately during their free time, and farmers who take jobs in factories while continuing the operation of their farms. Holders of second jobs average about twelve hours a week at their second jobs, which brings their average weekly worktime total to 52 hours. The term *moonlighting* is a misnomer. Only 32 per cent of second jobholders work at night; 44 per cent work during the usual weekday hours from morning to late afternoon, and 24 per cent work on the weekends.[5]

This increased incidence of moonlighting has become a source of concern for management. Spokesmen for industry decry the practice for a number of reasons.[6] Some managers suspect that the moonlighter is less productive and more accident prone than the non-moonlighter. Other managers believe that the absentee rate is unusually high among moonlighters. Farmers are conspicuous by their absence during the busy seasons of sowing, harvesting, and hunting; some moonlighters have been caught working at their second jobs while on a sick claims from their first jobs. Managers complain the loudest, however, when a man they have trained for a job moonlights with a competitor, leaking information and trade secrets to the latter. Holding two jobs is, consequently, grounds for discharge in many companies.

The labor unions are apparently as opposed to this practice as management groups.[7] Occasionally, they can trace their difficulty in organizing a shop to moonlighters, who fear that the union will pressure them to quit their jobs. The willingness of the moonlighter to work for less than union-approved wage rates is a source of dissatisfaction for union leaders. Some union leaders dislike the practice because they believe that the moonlighter is difficult to mobilize for union action.

Yet for all of the concern about this problem in labor and management groups and its prevalence in the population, we know very little about the moonlighter. How does he differ from the non-moonlighter in his personal values, his personality attributes, his self-esteem? What motivates him to take a second job? What social costs does the practice incur for him? To get the answers to these and other questions, the research outlined below was undertaken.

Methodology

In 1960 questionnaire data were collected from 1,076 blue-collar workers in continuous-process industries located in the middle-Atlantic states. This sample of workers was not selected on a probability basis. The primary interest was to study the effects of shift work on the worker.[8] As shift work is a particularly sensitive subject for management, research sites were selected from among the few companies or labor unions that would cooperate. Five plants were selected in two continuous-process industries.

One plant is located in one of the largest metropolitan areas in the United States; another is located in a city of over 100,000 population; two are located in urban centers of approximately 20,000 people; and the last site is in a rural area. The sample of respondents was selected systematically from lists of blue-collar workers provided by the company or by the union. The method of data collection varied at each site. Some of the questionnaires were distributed by sending members of the field staff to the workers' homes. Some questionnaires were collected at the plant, some at the union hall, and others by a return trip to the worker's home. The over-all response rate was 87 per cent, varying from 81 per cent at one site to 94 per cent at another. The incidence of moonlighting varied greatly from plant to plant depending on the shift pattern in the plant. In plants with rotating shifts, only 10 per cent of the workers reported that they had a second job. At another plant with the fixed shift pattern, the incidence of moonlighting rose to 28 per cent on the afternoon shift and 32 per cent on the night shift. These figures were well above the national average, but the conditions for moonlighting were unusually favorable in these communities.

Findings

There is no single explanation which accounts for every instance of moonlighting; the motivations of moonlighters are varied. A small proportion may take second jobs in order to escape an unpleasant marital situation. Others may simply enjoy their work. The person who identifies himself as an actor yet must work as a waiter because he cannot support himself from his infrequent appearances on the stage is another special case. But perhaps the most common motivation to moonlight arises from a complex set of conditions which impinge on the family's economic planning. Every family pursues a certain style of life as a goal and every style of life has its price tag. If the husband's wages are inadequate for obtaining the desired standard of living, then the family must make some decisions about how to proceed. One option is to reduce their economic aspirations. This recourse may be chosen if the husband feels physically incapable of taking a second job, if second jobs are not available, or if other conditions do not favor taking a second job. Another alternative is for the wife to take a job. This choice is often selected unless there are small children in the home. Moonlighting is another option.

The relationship between economic factors and multiple jobholding in the family is shown in Table 1. In terms of purchasing power the male workers in the four analysis categories earned approximately the same income from their first jobs, although the income of moonlighters whose wives do not work was the highest. However, in families where the husband has a second job or the wife was working, the debt level was higher and the income from the first job was

TABLE 1. BACKGROUND FACTORS AND MULTIPLE JOBHOLDING

	Do you have a second job?				
	Yes		No		
		Wife Working			
Background Factors	Yes	No	Yes	No	F Value
Percent completing high school or some college	50%	42%	39%	33%	6.17 p < .01
Average income of husband from his first job	$4,370	$4,600	$4,310	$4,460	3.92 p < .01
Average total family income	$6,000	$4,710	$6,100	$4,490	156.79 p < .01
Average debt size	$5,660	$4,680	$5,050	$4,080	4.55 p < .01
How adequate is your pay from your first job in helping you to pay your debts? (1 = not adequate at all)	2.53	2.77	2.80	3.02	4.47 p < .01
How worried are you about being able to pay your debts? (1 = not worried at all)	2.13	2.44	2.32	2.46	1.09 N.S.
Number of cases	38	98	245	566	

seen as less adequate for paying these debts. In 18 per cent of the families where the couple held a total of three jobs the debt level was in excess of $9,000. Since multiple jobholding increases the average family income by $250 to $1,640 per year, it enhances the ability of the family to handle its higher debt load. The higher levels of economic aspiration found in multiple job families are reflected in and are a partial consequence of the higher educational attainments of the husband. Almost one-half of the holders of two jobs completed high school and 7 per cent of them spent some time in college.

When a young married couple faces the problem of raising their income to achieve their economic aspirations, the usual course they follow is for the wife to get a job or to continue in the job she had before she married.[9] Almost one-half of the young wives (under 40 years of age) in our sample, who did not have children, were employed outside the home. These women, whether working part time or full time, contributed a little over one-quarter of the total family income (Table 1). This proportion is almost exactly the same as that found by M. S. Carroll in a study of the working wife using Bureau of Labor Statistics data.[10]

But once the couple has a child, the picture changes drastically. The wife is forced to withdraw from the labor force at least temporarily; less than 10 per cent of the young wives under 25 years of age continued to work outside the home during the first few years after they have had their first child. The couple faces an altered economic situation. The arrival of the child automatically increases the burden of necessary expenditures and, since the wife is no longer working, total family income declines. If the family had gone into debt in anticipation of continued income from both partners, the loss of the wife's income creates a vulnerable and anxious situation for the family.

It is at this juncture in the family cycle that the husband is likely to take a second job in order to maintain the family's level of living. Data from the Bureau of Labor Statistics show that 4.2 per cent of single men as compared with 7 per cent of married men had second jobs.[11] The incidence of moonlighting was highest for men between the ages of 25 and 44. The data from Table 2 permit a more detailed analysis of age, marital status, and the holding of a second job. As the table shows, the frequency of moonlighting increased with the age of the husband up to approximately age 35 and then tapered off until retirement. The wife, on the other hand, was likely to return to the job market after she was 35 years old, when her children were capable of caring for themselves. The effect that children have on parental work patterns is reflected in the fact that the frequency of moonlighting by husbands increased with the number of children in

TABLE 2. AGE AND MULTIPLE JOBHOLDING

	Age								
	21–25	26–30	31–35	36–40	41–45	46–50	51–55	56–60	61–65
Per cent of wives in the labor force	16%	24%	21%	25%	34%	38%	29%	21%	17%
Per cent of husbands with two jobs	11	16	18	17	15	13	12	5	5
Number of cases	54	83	98	132	180	174	130	76	49

the family. The wife, on the other hand, was less likely to be working as the number of children increased. The data on age and number of children suggest, therefore, that a certain complementarity exists between moonlighting and wife working. The care with which these activities often are articulated is reflected in one more finding. In two-thirds of the families where the wife was working and there were children at home, the parents worked different shifts so that one of them could always be at home with the children.

For all of their extra effort to meet their financial obligations, the moonlighters seem to find no solace in lessened worry about their ability to pay their debts. The data in Table 1 show no significant differences among the various groups on this dimension.

Marital Happiness

The problems in the division of labor and of coordination are undoubtedly greater in the multiple jobholding family. If the husband is working at two jobs, some of the household tasks which are traditionally ascribed to the husband role must be assumed by the wife. She may accept them willingly, even volunteering to perform them, or she may accept them reluctantly after arguments with her husband. Sometimes she may refuse to do them at all. If the wife is working, the husband may be expected to assume the responsibility for some of the activities usually ascribed to the role of wife. This process of adjustment may also be marked with tension and conflict between the partners, which results in reduced marital happiness. Following this reasoning, R. Blood, Jr., and R. Hamblin found that marital happiness was adversely affected by the strains induced by multiple jobholding.[12]

Our data do not support their findings. As long as there were less than three jobs in the family, marital happiness was unaffected. The responses of moonlighters whose wives worked indicated a tendency toward lower marital happiness in two of the measures, but this difference is significant only between the .05 and .10 levels. A preliminary analysis of the determinants of marital happiness sheds some light on the lack of relationship between multiple jobholding and marital happiness. Marital happiness is a core attitude which is not as easily affected by interactions between the husband and the wife as it is by the personality characteristics and symmetry of values of the partners. If these latter factors are favorable, interpersonal tension and conflict must be persistent and extreme before marital happiness is affected.

The Values of Moonlighters

A series of questions was designed to determine the kinds of role activities that our respondents valued.[13] The analysis of these data, as shown in Table 4, does not support the contention that moon-

TABLE 3. MARITAL HAPPINESS AND MULTIPLE JOBHOLDING

	Do you have a second job?				
	Yes		No		
	Wife Working				
Measures of Marital Happiness	Yes	No	Yes	No	F Value
How happily married are you? (1 = very happy)	2.18	1.87	1.82	1.84	1.73 N.S.
How often do you and your wife "get on each other's nerves"? (1 = never)	2.82	2.61	2.60	2.54	1.55 N.S.
Do you ever wish that you had not married? (1 = never)	1.85	1.62	1.59	1.62	0.89 N.S.
If you had your life to live over would you marry the same person? (1 = definitely)	1.91	1.80	1.83	1.83	0.08 N.S.
Number of cases	38	98	245	566	

lighters are more middle class in their role values than are other blue-collar workers. With the exception of two activity areas, moonlighters placed the same value on these important aspects of their roles as non-moonlighters. Husbands who had second jobs preferred to make the important family decisions themselves. The authoritarian preference is also reflected in another role activity not shown in the table: Moonlighters more than non-moonlighters preferred to handle the control and discipline of their children themselves. As we will see below, this inclination of the moonlighter is compatible with his personality need disposition for dominance.

The finding that husbands with one job whose wives were working were likely to put greater emphasis on being a helpmate to their wives is not surprising. The success of the family's income strategy

TABLE 4. IMPORTANCE OF ROLES AND MULTIPLE JOBHOLDING

	Do you have a second job?				
	Yes		No		
	Wife Working				
Role Areas[a]	Yes	No	Yes	No	F Value
Importance of being a companion to wife	3.21	3.29	3.53	3.43	1.01 N.S.
Importance of being a helpmate to wife	3.76	3.59	4.06	3.85	3.75 $p < .01$
Importance of teaching children skills	4.11	3.88	4.01	3.98	1.41 N.S.
Importance of being a pal to children	4.11	3.98	4.19	4.28	2.54 $p = .06$
Importance of having an equalitarian decision-making structure in the family	3.85	3.84	4.22	4.08	2.44 $p < .05$
Importance of having a full social life	2.61	2.32	2.28	2.36	0.82 N.S.
Number of cases	38	98	245	566	

[a] The higher the mean, the greater the importance of the role-area.

depends in part on the husband's willingness to assume responsibility for some of her activities.

The Self-Esteem of Moonlighters

Numerous studies have shown that the industrial worker is likely to undergo a period of cognitive readjustment after a few years on his primary job.[14] His aspirations of occupational mobility must be adjusted to the realities of the work situation with which he is becoming increasingly familiar. For the worker with a relatively high level of education, this adjustment must be particularly difficult because he is likely to have higher aspirations than less well-educated workers. Compounding the frustration is the fact that this change often occurs about the same time that increasing family size increases his debts. His evaluation of his performance—his self-esteem—as a worker and a family provider must suffer from this combination of circumstances. For some workers a second job becomes a way of achieving economic objectives after their mobility opportunities on their primary job have proved nonexistent.

To study the effects of these changes on the self-esteem of the worker, for his familial as well as his work roles, several measures of self-esteem were designed.[15] The first entry in Table 5—*Success at his job*—shows that the self-esteem of the husband was significantly lower when the family was a multiple jobholding unit. An analysis of this self-esteem item in different categories of age of father and age of youngest child suggests that the self-esteem of moonlighters does not recover until the children have grown up and have left home.

The social costs of moonlighting are also evident in the relationships of the moonlighter with his wife. His longer working hours prevented him from performing as well as a helpmate to his wife as he thought he should.

The moonlighter was, as we saw in the data on his values, just as involved in his father role as the non-moonlighter. But his self-esteem as a father was quite low and, in view of the value that he placed on that role, it must be a source of considerable dissatisfaction to him. Further, if the husband was moonlighting and the wife was working too, the husband's self-esteem was relatively low on the dimensions of controlling his children and running the family. It must be remembered from our previous discussion that these workers also attached great importance to these roles. This situation must also be a source of dissatisfaction to the moonlighter.

Finally, the moonlighter whose wife also worked suffered reduced self-esteem on the dimension of popularity with friends ($p < .04$). The consequences of this problem will be discussed in the next section.

TABLE 5. SELF-ESTEEM AND MULTIPLE JOBHOLDING

Measures of self-esteem in various roles[a]	Do you have a second job?				
	Yes		No		
	Wife Working				
	Yes	No	Yes	No	F Value
Success at his job	2.91	3.12	3.14	3.36	2.77
					$p = .05$
Being a companion to wife	3.30	3.56	3.71	3.76	1.96
					N.S.
Being a helpmate to wife	3.51	3.43	3.88	3.82	3.99
					$p < .01$
Being able to spend time with children	2.97	2.97	3.37	3.52	5.77
					$p < .01$
Being able to control children	3.79	4.15	4.06	4.17	1.61
					N.S.
Running the family	3.47	3.71	3.78	3.93	3.44
					$p = .02$
Being popular	3.59	3.81	3.78	3.93	2.29
					$p < .04$
Number of cases	38	98	245	566	

[a] The higher the mean, the higher the self-esteem.

Organizational Memberships

As the problem of moonlighting becomes an increasing object of concern to social scientists, the prediction is bound to be made that the moonlighter is socially withdrawn because of the pressures of maintaining two or more jobs. Table 6 below shows that this is not the case. The multiple jobholder was not merely as active as the one-jobholder, he was more active in certain voluntary associations. People with second jobs were more likely to join fraternal organizations, civic and service organizations, PTAs, and charitable and welfare organizations. In fact, more of them (22 per cent) managed to find time to be officers in their organizations than did the non-moonlighters (14 per cent). They also tended to spend more hours per week in organizational activities.

TABLE 6. PARTICIPATION IN VOLUNTARY ASSOCIATIONS
AND MULTIPLE JOBHOLDING

Voluntary Associations	*Do you have a second job?*		X^2 level of significance[a]
	Per cent "Yes"	Per cent "No"	
Fraternal organizations	27%	18%	.02
Veteran's clubs	15	12	N.S.
Political clubs	10	6	.08
Civic and service organizations	12	5	.01
Organized sport teams	29	21	.05
Charitable or welfare organizations	11	6	.04
Parent-Teachers Association	30	19	.01
Number of cases	136	811	

[a] Chi-square tests of significance are used in this table instead of F-tests because the data are expressed as percentages rather than as mean scores.

The simplest explanation of this finding might be that the moonlighters were better educated than the non-moonlighters. In this case we could invoke the usual proposition relating education to rates of participation. Table 7 below shows that this is not the whole story either.

People with two jobs simply were more energetic than those with one job. It is this greater physical capacity that probably accounted for their getting more education, taking a second job, and maintaining their high levels of activity in voluntary associations. We scan the data almost in vain to find an area in which the people with more than one job were less active than those with only one job. Moon-

TABLE 7. EDUCATION, ORGANIZATIONAL MEMBERSHIPS,
AND MULTIPLE JOBHOLDING

	Per cent reporting two or more organizational memberships		
Education Level	Moonlighters	Non-moonlighters	X^2 level of significance[a]
8th grade or less	42% (32)	25% (260)	< .05
Some high school	52% (44)	35% (268)	< .05
Completed high school or more	65% (60)	44% (283)	< .05

[a] Chi-square tests of significance are used in this table instead of F-tests because the data are expressed as percentages rather than as mean scores.

lighters were less inclined than one-jobholders to watch television, garden, visit friends, and take naps, but they were just as inclined as the latter to hunt, fish, and build and fix things. So even during those hours when they might rest, they still elected less sedentary activities than non-moonlighters. In spite of this heavy schedule of activity, the moonlighter was just as healthy as the non-moonlighter (according to our measure of general health constructed from an extensive battery of self-report health items).

Personality Dimensions

Personality profiles were obtained for each of the respondents by incorporating R. Cattell's 16 PF test in our questionnaires.[16] The data from this test provide support at the psychological level of abstraction for the findings in the earlier sections of the chapter.

In view of the moonlighter's proclivities for joining voluntary associations, it is not too surprising that he tended to be more cyclothymic and surgent. Translating from the language of Cattell, the moonlighter was *relatively* warmer, more outgoing, and enthusiastic than the holder of a single job. (The word *relatively* is underlined because the scores of the respondents in this sample were skewed toward the aloof and withdrawn end of the scale. Therefore, while the average scores of the moonlighters were significantly higher than those of non-moonlighters, they were only average for the working class when compared with a national sample of respondents involving all social classes.) The moonlighter's higher score on the dominance factor provides a motivational explanation for our finding that he desired to run his family and to control his children. The lower average score

TABLE 8.   PERSONALITY DIMENSIONS AND MULTIPLE JOBHOLDING

Measures of personality dimensions	Moonlighters	Non-moonlighters	T-test[a]
Cyclothymia-schizothymia	3.93[b]	3.65	p < .05
Surgency-desurgency	4.46	3.67	p < .01
Dominance-submission	5.26	4.63	p < .01
Premsia-harria	3.71	4.22	p < .01
(High-low) ergic tension	4.32	4.87	p < .01
(High-low) anxiety	4.80	5.02	p < .01
(High-low) resignation	5.37	5.87	p < .01
(High-low) neuroticism	4.89	5.14	p < .01
Number of cases	136	811	

[a] T-tests replace F-tests for these data because pairs rather than sets of four mean scores are being tested for significance.

[b] The higher the mean score, the greater the left characteristic listed in each row.

of the moonlighter on the premsia-harria factor suggests that the moonlighter was more practical, realistic, masculine, and independent than the non-moonlighter. The moonlighter suffered less from anxiety than the non-moonlighter. He was likely to have greater emotional stability. His positive and assertive outlook on life is reflected in his lower score on the resignation measure.

This syndrome of psychological traits and the higher levels of physical energy which characterized the moonlighters undoubtedly helps us to account for his choice of coping strategies. Faced with a disparity between his economic aspirations and his achievements, he upgrades his performance rather than reducing his aspirations.

Summary and Conclusions

The prevalence of moonlighting in our society is increased by the convergence of certain social and personal conditions. First, sufficient free time must be available for additional jobs and income. The trend toward the shorter workweek, therefore, is a major factor in accounting for the increasing prevalence of moonlighting in our society. Second, if shift work is prevalent in the community, the worker has increased opportunity to select a second job from among the more abundant daytime jobs while he works a second or third shift at his primary job. Third, if the community does not provide adequate opportunities for the leisure use of free time, the inclination to moonlight is probably increased. Fourth, whenever the three conditions just mentioned are favorable, those people in the population who have relatively high economic needs or aspirations will be inclined to take second jobs rather than reducing their aspirations. There are other reasons for moonlighting—e.g., marital difficulties— but economic aspirations which exceed achievements on the first job are felt to be the most common motivation for taking a second job. Fifth, the possession of high aspirations is not enough for sustained moonlighting; the worker must have adequate physical energy and the appropriate psychological traits if he is to be a successful moonlighter. Aspiration theories which assume that the physical energies of individuals match their aspirations miss an important factor in accounting for behavioral differences.

Moonlighting is usually the second alternative for the family that wishes to augment its income. Until the couple has children, the wife is likely to go to work or to keep her old job. While these solutions do handle the problem of maintaining the desired style of life, they may have negative effects on the self-esteem of the worker. Certainly the husband suffers from reduced self-esteem in roles that he values at least as highly as the non-moonlighter. He cannot relate to his wife, his children, or his friends in the ways that he would like to relate to them.

There are probably three key characteristics that distinguish the moonlighter from the non-moonlighter: (1) his personality profile, (2) his physical capacity for activity, and (3) his higher levels of economic aspirations. He is surgent, dominant, tough-minded, and not easily given to resignation. He is so energetic that he can maintain two jobs, be active in voluntary associations, and still shun the other more sedentary leisure activities of the non-moonlighter in favor of the more vigorous ones.

Notes

1. P. E. Mott, F. C. Mann, Q. McLoughlin, and D. Warwick, *Shift Work: The Social, Psychological, and Physical Consequences*, Ann Arbor, Mich., The University of Michigan Press, 1965.

2. S. de Grazia, *Of Time, Work, and Leisure*, New York, Twentieth Century Fund, 1962.

3. H. Swados, "Less Work—Less Leisure," in *Mass Leisure*, E. Larrabee and R. Meyerson, eds., New York, The Free Press of Glencoe, 1958, pp. 353–363.

4. F. Panzer, "The Moonlighters," *Industrial Bulletin*, September 1958, pp. 15–18; J. Schiffman, "Multiple Job Holders in May, 1962," *Monthly Labor Review*, May 1963, pp. 516–523.

5. J. Schiffman, *op. cit.*

6. L. Stessin, "Free Enterprise by Moonlight," *Dun's Review and Modern Industry*, July 1959, pp. 47–49; "Moonlighting in the Office," Survey of the Month, *American Business Magazine*, January 1958, pp. 21–24; J. Meade, "The Two-Job Worker," *Canadian Business*, May 1958, p. 96; S. Habbe, "Moonlighting and Its Controls," *Management Record*, July 1957, pp. 234–236.

7. B. McClancy, "The Moonlighters," *For the Informed Executive*, September 1957, No. 212, pp. 1–4; B. McClancey, "Moonlighting," *For the Informed Executive*, January 1954, No. 125, pp. 5–8; "The Man With Two Jobs," *Fortune*, November 1961, pp. 211–216.

8. Mott, *et al., op. cit.*

9. The same cautionary note must be made about the motivations for the wife's acceptance of a job as was made about the husband's decision to take a second job; while economic needs and aspirations are undoubtedly the major motivations, escape from marital difficulties, relief from boredom, desire to use creative abilities, etc., are also factors in the decisions of many wives.

10. M. S. Carroll, "The Working Wife and Her Family's Economic Position," *Monthly Labor Review*, April 1962, pp. 366–374.

11. Schiffman, *op. cit.*

12. R. Blood, Jr., and R. Hamblin, "The Effects of the Wife's Employment on the Family Power Structure," in *A Modern Introduction to the Family*,

N. Bell and E. Vogel, eds., New York, The Free Press of Glencoe, 1960, pp. 137–142.

13. Using the helpmate aspect of the husband role as an example, the following item illustrates the structure of the centrality questions:

Bill Thinks:
A man's wife can't help him with his work, she should get her own work done, so he doesn't have to work some more with her when he gets home.

Al Thinks:
When a man's around he should help out. She has a long hard job taking care of the house and the kids, and he should share the load.

| I'm like Bill | I'm more like Bill than like Al | I'm halfway between Bill and Al | I'm more like Al than like Bill | I'm like Al |

14. "Job Attitudes: Review of Research and Opinion," *Bulletin of the Psychological Service of Pittsburgh:* Report No. 2, ed. by F. Herzberg and D. Capevell, Psychological Service of Pittsburgh, 1955.

15. A sample self-esteem item:

Art Thinks:
Art feels pretty happy about the way he's helped his wife out with things. She has a pretty tough job, and he's done a lot to make things easier for her. He's taken her out to get her away from the work, and he's pitched in and helped when he could. All in all, this makes him feel pretty good.

Ted Thinks:
Ted feels pretty unhappy about the amount of extra work he's made for his wife. A lot of times he has upset her schedule. He hasn't done much to make things easier for her, either by helping with the work, or by getting her away from it. As he looks back, this makes him feel pretty bad.

| I'm like Art | I'm more like Art than like Ted | I'm halfway between Art and Ted | I'm more like Ted than like Art | I'm like Ted |

16. R. Cattell, *Handbook Supplement for Form C of the Sixteen Personality Factor Test,* Champaign, Ill., Institute for Personality and Ability Testing, 1962, 2nd ed.

6. The Economics of Overtime

FREDERIC MEYERS

Graduate School of Business Administration
University of California, Los Angeles

The word overtime contains implicitly the notion that some kind of norm exists against which worktime worked or offered may be measured. Work in excess of this norm is "overtime." For reasons that must be purely conventional, the norm is usually expressed in terms of daily or weekly hours, or daily hours for a specified number of days per week.[1] In the United States, as well as in most other industrial countries, the fact that hours worked are "overtime" is usually identifiable by the payment of a premium rate. Great variation exists from bargain to bargain, industry to industry, and country to country as to the conditions under which premium rates are paid, and their level under a wide variety of possible conditions.

Conventional wage analysis usually ignores the existence of this complex set of practices. Their careful examination, concentrating on the phenomena of interest to the economist, using the tools and method of economic analysis is, I think, interesting and rewarding to the economist and perhaps to others. The first part of this chapter will attempt to deal, in the conventional static form, with these purely economic problems. The model used to analyze the wage and em-

95

ployment effects of premium overtime practices, using static economic analysis, is not, as economic models go, particularly complex. To noneconomists, the analysis may seem confusing and unduly formal. But an essay on the economics of overtime must concern itself with these problems and techniques. To any reader, the conclusions at least may be of interest.

The second and shorter portion of the chapter deals briefly with the longer run dynamics of the problem. Unfortunately, this section, as a result of the way I see the problem, is much less precise and more speculative. For the same reasons, it is much less highly formal and less like the conventional economic analysis.

The Pure Theory of Overtime

The institution of premium rates for work beyond a specified number of hours per day or per week will affect the supply of labor in a labor market. For purposes of simplicity, this analysis will deal with the problem assuming

1. That all workers work the same number of hours per week; that is, in effect, the part-time component of the labor force is ignored

2. That no significant distinctions need be made whether premium rates are paid on a daily or on a weekly basis.

I wish, then, to compare two supply functions of labor in which average hourly earnings are related to the total number of hours of work offered per week in a labor market. The first supply function assumes no premium overtime rule—all hours paid for, from the first to the last, are paid at a constant hourly rate. The second assumes that hours worked past some specified number, n, are paid for at some multiple, $k > 1$, times the straight-time rate.

Let us assume, as in Figure 1, a function which expresses the willingness of a typical worker to work varying number of hours per week related to varying weekly incomes. For the purposes of this discussion, we will assume this function to be positively sloped throughout. This function appears as ss. Related to it is a function,

FIGURE 1

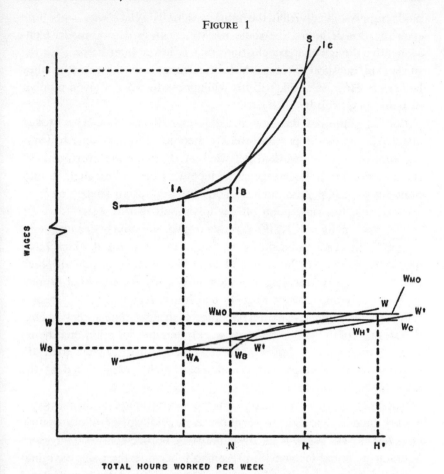

TOTAL HOURS WORKED PER WEEK

ww, which expresses for each hypothetical weekly income a wage rate. At each wage rate, this function defines the marginal weekly income to the worker for each hour worked.

Now suppose the market sets a wage rate W, at which the worker will be willing to work H hours, producing a weeking income of I. Suppose further that subsequently an overtime rule is established providing that after n hours per week, a premium rate kW must be paid. Suppose finally that the market initially sets a new wage rate such that for H hours, the same weekly earnings can be made. Consequently, though the straight-time rate is lower than before, for the worker in question, average hourly earnings are the same as they had been. How, if at all, will his willingness to work a given number of hours per week be changed?

Let W_s represent the new straight time hourly rate. The broken line $I_a I_b I_c$ represents possible weekly incomes corresponding to varying number of hours worked per week at W_s given the overtime rule. By assumption, it intersects ss at income I. As illustrated, it may intersect at two points, but will not, with any usual shapes of ss, if W_s is higher than any point on ww to the left of n.

The broken line $W_a W_b W_c$ represents average hourly earnings corresponding to each point on $I_a I_b I_c$. Since at each point at which $I_a I_b I_c$ intersects ss, weekly income and weekly hours are equal on each function, the corresponding average hourly earnings are equal, so that $W_a W_b W_c$ intersects ww at wage W and hours H. The line W_{mo} represents the premium rate corresponding to straight time rate W_s, and, therefore, represents the marginal weekly income for additional hours worked in excess of hours n. W_{mo} is necessarily greater than W, since W is an average, some hours of which were worked at the lower straight-time rate.

The worker now is faced with the opportunity, with the same weekly income and hourly earnings as previously, of offering more or fewer hours. Without an overtime rule, he declined to offer more hours at marginal income W, presumably because the rising marginal utility of leisure and disutility of work passed the declining marginal utility of income at hours H and income I.[2] But now the marginal weekly income W_{mo} is higher than before. It can safely be assumed that the worker will be willing to offer more hours at straight-time rate W_s with the premium rate after n hours than he had before at wage rate W without the premium, even though at those hours he had previously worked, average hourly earnings and weekly income are the same.

At any new number of hours larger than H, however, average hourly earnings defined by the line portion $W_b W_c$ are lower than WW; that is, lower than the wage required to be offered without an overtime rule to call forth H weekly hours. Therefore, at the straight-time rate W_s with the premium rate the worker will offer more hours than he would at wage W without the overtime rule, but the resulting hourly earnings will be less than W. Precisely how many additional hours will be offered, and therefore the level of the new hourly earnings will depend upon the utility functions for work, leisure, and income.

Suppose the new number of hours offered to be H', producing average hourly earnings of $W'_{h'}$. For each hypothetical market wage a corresponding point exists representing the weekly hours offerings of the worker at the related straight-time wage rate with an overtime rule. Connecting these points gives the function $_{w'w'}$ which lies to the right of ww. This function begins slightly to the right of hours n, since for hours less than n the premium rate does not apply, and ww expresses the hourly rates which will call forth only some number of hours less than n.

Thus, for each possible hourly earnings in excess of a wage about equal to that required to produce n hours, there are two responses from the worker. One supposes that the hourly earnings are composed only of payments at constant rates without regard to hours; the other that they are composed of an average of hours worked at straight-time and at overtime premium rates. The former produces fewer hours, the latter more. The size of the kink at n hours and the slope of $w'w'$ depends on the size of the premium k. The higher the premium, the farther $w'w'$ is to the right of ww.

To produce supply functions for labor under these two possible conditions, the individual supply functions, ww and $w'w'$, may be cumulated, and the necessary adjustments made for changes in labor force participation rates as earnings opportunities may vary. These functions appear on Figure 2. SRS' represents the supply function assuming no premium overtime rule. SS represents the adjusted portion of the supply function with an overtime rule. It shows the kink at approximately point *R,* the point at which the hypothetical wage produces from workers about the number of hours, *n,* at which the premium rate begins. The two functions show that in a labor market at a given hourly wage, more hours will be offered at each wage in excess of that corresponding to *R* when the hourly wage has a pre-

FIGURE 2

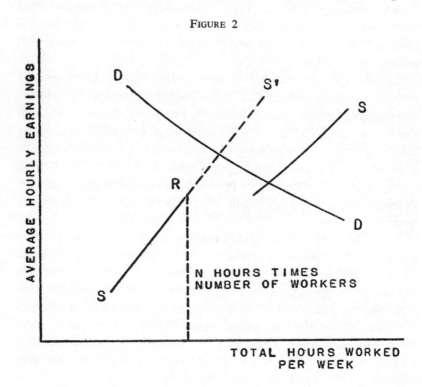

mium rate component—that is, a lower straight-time rate but some hours at the higher premium—than if the offer is for any number of hours at a constant hourly rate.

The analysis thus far is predicated upon a positively sloped labor supply function. If, in all or some portions, labor supply is negatively sloped, the effect of the imposition of an overtime rule depends on the underlying reasons for the shape. A negative slope may result from family characteristics and attitudes toward income, or from the relatively high value that the individual places on leisure as against additional income, so that as the rate of wages rises more leisure is taken.

If family characteristics are the principal reason for the negative slope—that is, if as individual wage incomes rise, secondary workers tend to withdraw from the labor force—high premium overtime rates may result in the more rapid withdrawal of members of the family other than the primary wage earner. Looking at the family as a unit in its function as a supplier of labor, its income goals may be more readily reached by the offering of relatively few overtime hours by the primary wage earner than by the entry or continuance into the labor force of the wife or potential young wage earners; that is, one may look at work offerings as successive, the family substituting labor of secondary wage earners after the net utility of additional work of the primary earner becomes negative. Raising the rate of remuneration of additional hours for the primary wage earner may postpone the entry of possible secondary workers, who would earn only straight-time rates for the beginning hours.

However, if a substantial reason for the negative slope is the rapidly declining preference for income over leisure, premium overtime rates would still result in the kind of kink noted above and shifting of a portion of the supply curve to the right. The rule still produces more income for the same sacrifice of leisure at the point at which overtime rates begin.

If the demand function for labor (*DD* in Figure 2) cuts the alternate supply functions above point *R*, equilibrium employment measured by total weekly hours is greater and equilibrium average hourly wages are lower with an overtime rule than without. The analogy might be with a reverse auction-type market, in which the employer is buying the cheapest hours first, then paying only the higher rate for the marginal high-priced hours. While the conclusion that the imposition of an overtime rule may reduce average hourly earnings may seem at first glance startling, that it increases offerings of work is common sense, and the second conclusion follows from the first.

Given tight labor markets, then, the imposition of an overtime rule, by law or custom or collective agreement, may result in lower average wages and more hours worked than would be the case if all hours were paid for at a uniform hourly rate.

Thus, in time of war, proposals to suspend the operation of the overtime provisions of the Fair Labor Standards Act were almost certainly mistaken, both from the point of view of public policy as well as from the narrow cost viewpoint of the individual employer. The opportunity to work overtime at premium rates probably produced more hours worked at lower average cost than would have been the case if premium rates had been abolished, but average earnings permitted to rise to those levels available with the premium arrangement.

Now suppose that by union or legislative action, not only is it required that premium overtime rates be paid for hours in excess of n, but that employers are required to pay a straight-time wage higher than that corresponding to point R. Since workers then may not offer to work at wages less than the minimum and cannot work at straight time rates for hours in excess of n, the effective labor supply function becomes $S''R'S'''S$ in Figure 3; that is, it is horizontal at the minimum wage to n hours times the number of workers. It then slopes upwards until it meets SS, the slope depending upon the rates of overtime premium and reflecting the effect of the premium on average hourly earnings.

Now assume a demand for labor, DD, such that the equilibrium with an overtime rule but without the minimum wage is W, and the equilibrium wage assuming no overtime rule and no minimum wage would have been W'. The equilibrium with the minimum wage and overtime rule will be W''.

If this analysis is correct, it suggests some interesting conclusions concerning the impact of minimum wage and overtime rules imposed either by union action or by the law if the relationship of the several functions be those described in Figure 3. Suppose the relationship of the demand, the supply before the imposition of the overtime rule, and the supply after the overtime rule to be such that the over-

FIGURE 3

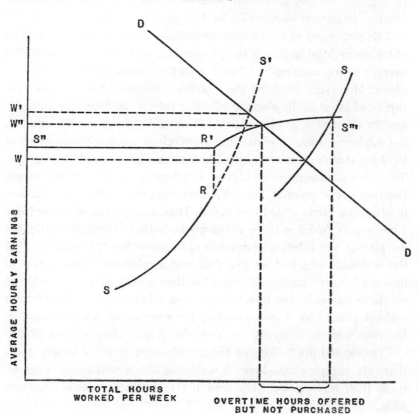

time rule in a context of full employment has some effect, in that employers elect to offer some overtime employment. In terms of the model, this means that the demand function cuts the supply functions above point *R*. If then a minimum wage rate is imposed above wage *W*—that is, the wage is above what it would have been with the overtime rule alone—average hourly earnings may be below what they would have been without either rule, and employment greater, though some "unemployment" may appear. This unemployment, however, is largely overtime hours offered but not purchased. This will be the case for any minimum wage such that $R'S'''$ cuts the demand function below the intersection of DD and SS'.

This may seem to be a highly unrealistic situation, where the effect of union or legal action is to set overtime and wage rules such that average hourly earnings are below what they would have been without either. However, consider the possible evidence. Suppose SS', the supply of labor in the absence of either rule, to be relatively inelastic, and/or demand relatively elastic. Then, if W'' is above W'—that is, the minimum wage is above the equilibrium wage without union or legal interference—no or negligible overtime hours would be worked. This case is illustrated in Figure 4. Likewise, if DD cut the supply function below point R, though a minimum wage might be effective, no overtime hours would be offered. Thus, always assuming the basic labor supply function to be relatively inelastic or demand elastic, the working of any substantial number of overtime hours is evidence that the combined effect of an overtime and a minimum wage rule is to increase hourly earnings above what they would have been with an overtime rule only, but to set them below what they would have been without either. As a consequence, the number of hours worked is less than with the overtime rule only, but greater than without either.[3]

Complicated discussions of the actual shape of labor supply functions are inappropriate here; however, it is not unreasonable to assume that, realistically, they tend not to be highly elastic, market-wide.

One final comment on the implications of the model, though referred to once, seems worth reiterating and generalizing. Conventional analyses of the impact of minimum wage rules on employment often tend to emphasize the disemployment effects. Though these depend on the shapes of the demand-and-supply functions,[4] it is never clear whether any unemployment which may result in complete unemployment of individuals, widespread part-time employment defined as weekly or annual work schedules less than those conventionally defined by usual overtime rules, or the failure to sell overtime hours

FIGURE 4

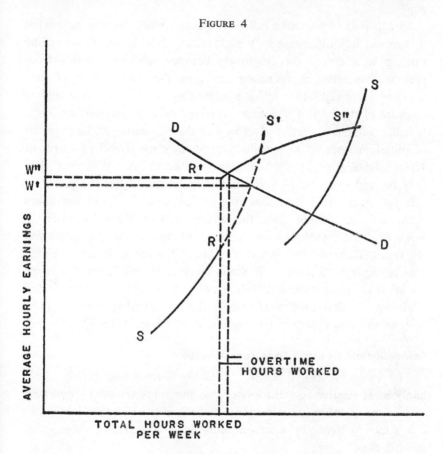

offered at prevailing rates. While the last may be defined by the price economist as "unemployment," it would certainly not be considered unemployment worth bothering about from a public policy point of view.

It is my belief that conventional analyses of the impact of unions or minimum-wage legislation on wages and employment with the tools of price economics have failed to account for the effects of overtime rules. The above analysis is an initial attempt to fill this gap.

In a period of less than full employment, while there is no reason to suppose any difference in the character of labor supply, overtime rules pose a choice for employers between additional hours from present employees at premium rates, or the employment of new workers at straight time. The straight-time rate is not a complete measure of the cost of new hires—hiring, training, and certain fringe benefits costs are a partial offset against the alternative of the payment of premium rates. A recent study provides some useful measures of these relationships in the contemporary economy.[5] Whatever they may be, there can be no serious doubt that the higher the premium rate required, either by union rule or law, and the fewer the hours permissible at straight time, the greater will be the substitution of work of the unemployed for work at premium rates by employed workers. Whatever the extent of this substitution, if an overtime rule is required to produce it, some increase in unit labor costs may be inferred, since presumptively employers would have substituted additional workers for additional hours of existing workers even without the rule if such a course would have been efficient.

Some Observations on Long-run Dynamics

The foregoing is, of course, a highly formal and purely static analysis. It neglects certain longer run functions served by overtime rules. One of the more important of these is to crystallize into practice social preferences between more income and more leisure as income rises.

It is a commonplace that as the potential of a society to produce goods and services rises, a part of the increase in satisfaction is likely to be taken in increased leisure. This has certainly been the history in the United States.[6] But the mechanics of exercising this choice are different and not so ready as, for example, the mechanics of enforcing a consumer choice between different goods and services. In the latter case, choices may be effectively exercised in such small individual units as to be reasonably regarded as infinitesimal; in the former, choices cannot effectively be made individually. The technological imperative requires that they be made at least by finite productive or managerial units. Consumption patterns may be infinitely various; work schedule patterns must generally be uniform within a productive unit.[7]

Thus, within any productive unit, changes in hours of work tend to lag behind changes in the preferences of employees. For any kind of change to take place by individual bargaining is virtually impossible, at least, unless, and until strong and unanimous choices for shorter hours appear. There is simply no effective way for changed preferences to express themselves individually.

Within American institutional arrangements, only the law or the device of collective bargaining provides a way of producing change in hours of work when this is the predominant though not universal choice, and only such devices provide a machinery through which an effective decision representing a central tendency of varying individual desires may be effectuated quickly. And the law requires greater uniformity of action, and therefore less adaptability to varying desires of individuals, as both their incomes and their preferences vary, than does the device of collective bargaining.

Thus, overtime rules are commonly established by collectivities. Changed standards tend to be set by individual collective bargains, often hotly disputed. They then spread to satellite bargains, and to unorganized segments of the economy.[8]

With several major exceptions, the law has played little initiating role in the United States. The example of the federal government in establishing an eight-hour day for its employees around the turn of the century played a significant crystallizing role. Certainly the Fair Labor Standards Act of 1938 had a major impact. It was preceded by the Walsh-Healey Act requiring premium overtime after 40 hours for federal contractors. Other relevant state and federal legislation should be mentioned, but in general patterns have been set by private, collective negotiation rather than by law.

As mentioned previously, this is probably preferable so as to permit adaptability to a greater range both of preferences and of technical limitations. And the device of the premium rate serves as a financial deterrent to the employer, while permitting the working of overtime when it is worth the cost, as compared with the alternatives.

But the establishment of overtime rules and their patent tendency to move toward cross-industry uniformity serves not only to reflect individual preferences and lead them to some kind of central tendency; they serve also to focus and crystallize inchoate and diverse individual desires into social norms and goals. Like the wage goals of American workers, their leisure goals can best be specified with Samuel Gompers' monosyllable, "more." How much more, or how much less, work for what weekly income probably cannot be made precise, even by the individual.

Formal overtime rules serve, then, not only to provide the possibility of change by substituting plantwide rules for futile individual attempts to negotiate possibly varying individual work schedules. They serve also to create preferences and make them more nearly uniform. There can be no doubt that though individual overtime rules result from the interplay of individual wishes to reduce hours and increase earnings, of employer preferences to contain or reduce labor costs,[9] and of technological demands, overtime rules influence individual norms after their adoption. As they become general they create social norms. We now believe hours of work should be in the neighborhood of 40 per week, though before the adoption of the Fair Labor Standards Act, judgments might have varied widely. This focusing of social norms is expressed in many ways. For example, in defining unemployment and employment, while we may count as partial unemployment hours offered in excess of those worked below 40 per week, failure to find opportunities to work at overtime rates will not be measured as partial unemployment any more than, for example, inability to find a moonlighting job by a "fully employed" person.

Having focused these social norms, during a period of unemployment, overtime rules then *do* serve as a device to distribute employment more consistently with the norm than might otherwise be done. They provide a measuring rod against which the concept of full-time employment may be set, and provide incentives to enforce conformity. In a period of full employment, the availability of overtime premium rates provides greater flexibility and adaptability to labor market pressures than would wage payment practices which excluded these rates. They permit the calling forth of additional labor through payment of the premium rate without the necessity of the upward adjustment of homogeneous hourly rates that would be necessary to bring an equivalent number of additional hours into the market. They also permit employers to get the desired additional hours without freezing into the wage structure a higher base rate which might be subject to the familiar downward rigidities.

For these reasons, then, the overtime rule seems to me to be a very useful social invention which contributes in a variety of ways to the solution of important social and economic problems. This does not say that the particular variants of the rule adopted in a particular time or place, among the infinite variety possible, are best, necessarily. A statement of the criteria for this "best choice" is dealt with by Melvin Reder in Chapter 11.

It would be extraordinarily difficult, perhaps impossible, to devise a purely economic model to predict the combination of base rates, hours of work after which overtime begins, and premium-rate structure which will result from any particular concatenation of economic forces. The existence of "overtime unemployment"—that is, of offers to work at premium rates that are not taken up—is evidence of disequilibrium of some kind. However, since adjustments can result in any one, or more than one, of the three variables—base rates, "normal" hours, and the premium structure—the solution would seem clearly to be indeterminate.

But more important, the variables normally considered to be independent, individual choices, are themselves conditioned sharply by the overtime conventions adopted as a result of bargaining and legislative processes. These bargaining choices, taken in an environment of varying and indecisive individual preferences, and in finite, often large, units, do not merely reflect established norms but help to establish them.

Notes

1. This convention is not universal. In the railroad industry, for example, monthly mileage limitations for engine service employees have been the device. In some seasonal industries and under some guaranteed wage plans, annual hours with flexible daily or weekly conventions serve as norms. These achieve sanction in the Fair Labor Standards Act.

2. For an analysis and review of the literature on this problem see Clyde E. Dankert, "Shorter Hours—In Theory and Practice," *Industrial and Labor Relations Review*, XV, No. 2 (April 1962).

3. This analysis neglects the effect of fixed fringe benefit costs per employee. But see Joseph W. Garbarino, "Fringe Benefits and Overtime as Barriers to Expanding Employment," *Industrial and Labor Relations Review*, XVII, No. 3 (April 1964).

4. See my paper, "Price Theory and Union Monopoly," *Industrial and Labor Relations Review*, XII, No. 3 (April 1959).

5. *Ibid.*

6. See Ethel B. Jones, "New Estimates of Hours of Work per Week and Hourly Earnings, 1900–1957," *Review of Economics and Statistics*, XLV, No. 4 (November 1963).

7. There are, of course, some exceptions. Outside salesmen can, for example, vary their schedules individually, accepting the earnings consequences of doing so. In the cast iron pipe industry, while a nominal workday exists, molders may often leave upon the completion of a task. In the transit or railroad industries, the normal workday may vary individually with the scheduled length of a run, but here, of course, the schedule establishes certain parameters within which individual work schedules must be set. Other examples could be mentioned.

8. Historically, as in pensions and certain other fringe benefits, targets were often set in office and managerial positions. Here managers were able effectively to express their own preferences and found it convenient to extend them to employees closely associated with them. Contemporarily, the lead is taken more often by organized groups.

9. The employer interest, in terms of our model, would be a complex set of premiums that bought each successive hour at the wage just sufficient to call it forth. Employers then would be capturing all of the something analogous to Marshall's consumer surplus.

7. Shift Work and the Shorter Workweek*

FLOYD C. MANN

Institute for Social Research
The University of Michigan

Hours of work have long been recognized as having a marked effect on the way an individual and his family lives. Perhaps the first workweek was established with the biblical injunction that man should not work more than six days. The workday may have evolved even earlier. Man's very body rhythms are geared to the diurnal regularities of the planetary system of which he is a part. It has long been observed that the day-and-night cycle of our planet underpins the principal pattern of work, play, and sleep that governs the lives of most people.

The six-day workweek and the workday from sun up to sun down were basic societal patterns that were unchanged for most of our recorded history. It is only relatively recently—with the coming of the industrial revolution—that the conventions about hours of work

* The research reported in this chapter was conducted under a grant (M–3276) from the National Institutes of Health, U.S. Public Health Service, Bethesda, Maryland.

began to be altered. As man in the West began to develop his skills of observation and analysis and to understand more and more of the regularities in his world, new knowledge came into existence. This knowledge led to technological innovations and the applications of these innovations to industry. These advances in technology and industry in turn began to change the daily life of the worker, his hours of work, and his workweek.

These are societal processes which have not yet run their full course. At mid-twentieth century the American society continues to be an increasingly scientific society. As more is spent each year on research and development, and this is translated into new technology, we learn more of the advantages and disadvantages of greater and greater industrialization. Each year more of our productive systems become mechanized, further rationalized, and developed into continuous flow process systems. Moreover, what is envisaged as the cybernation revolution is scarcely under way.[1] Man is learning to adapt himself to a scientific, rational, machine-based, changing society. The working of shifts is a part of this adaptation.

The social and economic forces within the industrial revolution that first led to changes in the hours of work continue to force us to try and think through what is the optimum allocation of time to work. Moreover, as we have begun to recognize that what is optimum for the society may not be optimum for the individual—and we gain more knowledge about the costs and benefits of different patterns of working hours—we find hours of work is truly a problem worthy of considerable attention. The work schedule affects the well-being of both the society and its individual member.

The centrality of hours of work to the effectiveness of a society is best seen by looking at the effects of markedly different schedules of hours than the predominant pattern of work from morning to late afternoon that most of us know so intimately and to which we are so accustomed. The study of the consequences of different patterns of shift work provides many insights into how our society functions. This is one of the principal reasons why a small group of us recently focused our research energies on the effects of shift work.[2] As it became increasingly clear to us that shift work would continue to be a requirement for many workers manning blue- and white-collar work flows, and as it became more evident that the demands of these odd-hour work schedules pose conflicts for the individual between meeting his body needs for rest and predictability and his social needs as a husband, father, and friend, we undertook a study to investigate the social, psychological, and physical consequences of different work schedules. This study has provided us with some insights into the effects of different schedules of work that may be relevant to present debate about whether to shorten the workweek.

Shift Work: A Concomitant of an Industrial Society

Historical economists note that shift work—working during some span of time each day other than the usual hours from morning to evening—first began to occur when factory owners found that by extending the operation of their machinery over more hours per day they could spread the cost of their capital investment to more units of production and reduce costs. Thus, as new knowledge has resulted in more complex technology and greater capital investments have been required, there has been ever greater demand to operate around the clock. This economic-accounting fact is the basic reason why we find evening and night shifts in manufacturing plants even where there are no continuous flow processing requirements as in the steel, chemical, and paper plants for 24-hour, seven-day-week operations. In the continuous process plants it is, of course, the nature of the materials that first requires the productive process to be uninterrupted. Daily shut-downs and start-ups are not possible. The procedures for putting "a catcracker," an open hearth furnace, or a synthetic fiber plant "on-line" or taking it "off-stream" are too complicated, time consuming, and costly to permit these operations to function less than continuously. In both of these types of plants shift work has become an increasingly common requirement.

More recently the major breakthrough in the theory and technology of information, communication, and control set the stage for another surge of changes in the productive processes, the organization of work, and the manning of plants and offices—and for continuing the demand that some people work shifts. Assembly-line manufacturing processes requiring large numbers of workers deployed at work stations all along engine lines were made obsolete as it became possible to move engine blocks by more highly mechanized transfer equipment and to drill holes for cylinders by complex, self-monitoring machine tools. With greater mechanization, fewer men were needed on the lines—fewer men were required to work evening or night shifts. The development of servo-mechanisms so that machines rather than men could control even more of the process in the continuous process industries also led toward smaller work forces—and fewer shift workers—monitoring more of the process.

Closely related to these technological changes in the factory and the plant were analogous changes in the office. New electronic data processing equipment began cutting into the increasing need for white-collar workers. However, greater capital investment in office equipment per man began the press toward operating more hours each day there too. Small cadres of white-collar workers were asked to work second and third shifts to optimize the use of computer systems. Thus, while fewer men were needed to operate more complex equipment systems in both the plant and the office, some clerical workers were beginning to work the "odd hour" shifts by the late 1950s and the early 1960s.

What will be the effect of these trends on the number of people who work shifts? It is not certain. It is not yet clear that the aggregate number of people working shifts will be greater or smaller in the future than when our productive processes were less automated. There is, however, no question that shift work will continue to be a fact in the daily lives of many workers and their families in the United States.[3] This appears to be demanded by the economics of the situation. The assumptions on which our cost accounting procedures are based are primarily economic. The economic gains that accrue from 24-hour operation more than offset the additional economic costs of wage differentials for shift workers or the additional costs of more errors and somewhat less output from the odd hour shifts.

One may be equally certain—considering the economic premises employed in cost accounting—that the businessman will not let expensive capital equipment stand idle should the standard present workweek be reduced.[4] Even changes in the rate of obsolescence press toward more shift work. Not only does new equipment cost more, but as the rate of obsolescence continues to rise, employers are forced to give greater attention to the feasibility of multiple shift operations.

It would appear then that shift work is a concomitant of an increasingly scientific and industrial society. The economics of greater and greater capital investment relative to the additional labor costs of around-the-clock operations almost dictates that segments of the work force will work shifts. Having noted some of the principal facts causing shift work, let us turn to what is known about the consequences of shift work.

Physical, Social, and Psychological Consequences of Shift Work

Most of what has been known concerning the effects of shift work has been derived from research that has been sporadic and highly segmented. Each major war with its need for greater production has produced a flurry of concern and writing about the effects of additional shifts on the work force. Most of the literature deals with personal experiences and solutions attempted in a specific plant; little is the product of careful and thorough investigation. When careful work has been done, the research has generally been highly focused and segmented. One researcher will be concerned with the organizational effects of shift work—the productivity of different shifts, differences in absence rates, in quality of product, errors, etc. Another will be concerned with the effects of shift work on the individual—his physical health, his feelings toward the world, and sense of well-being. Those

who focused on the worker's health were seldom equally concerned
with the effect of the shift work schedule on his family or opportunities to participate in the affairs of his community. Those who
investigated the social consequences rarely did anything very systematic in the study of psychological consequences. The orientations
and preoccupations of the different professions from which the researchers come are reflected in the gaps in our knowledge about the
noneconomic consequences of shift work.

A brief review of the findings from the more careful studies in this
literature is in order before presenting some of the facts from an
extensive study just completed in the United States.[5] At the outset
it is worth noting that most of the thorough work in this field has
been done in Europe. Moreover, most of the studies that are worker-
centered (rather than organization-centered) have tended to focus
on the employee's physical health. It is only recently that the effects
of the shift worker's schedule on his family and social participation,
and on his attitudes and affective states, have received systematic
consideration.

In the area of physiological effects there is a consensus that shift
work disrupts the time-oriented body functions of a sizable proportion
of workers. This literature indicates that many night and rotating
shift workers report trouble with basic rhythms of sleeping, eating,
and eliminating. Shift workers often have trouble getting to sleep
and staying asleep. They complain about the quality of their sleep.
They do not get as many hours of sleep when they work the night
shift. It is frequently noted that the changes in the job hours of shift
workers affect their appetite and digestion. Even more difficult to
change are the physiological rhythms involved in the elimination of
major wastes from the body.

When one turns from these disorders to the relationship between
work schedules and more serious health problems, like upper gastrointestinal disorders and general health complaints, there is less agreement among the researchers. E. Thiis-Evensen analyzed the complaints of workers who transferred from shift work to day work

and found that 30 per cent reported gastritis—problems more serious than appetite disturbances but less serious than ulcers.[6] V. Bjerner, A. Holm, and A. Swenssen found very little difference between shift workers and nonshift workers on either the frequency of consulting a physician or on the rate of hospitalization for stomach disorders until they divided the day workers into those who had previously worked shifts and those who had not.[7] Then they found significantly higher rates for the day workers who had formerly been on shift work.

Several European studies present evidence that rotating shift workers are more likely to complain of ulcers than fixed shift workers. A. Pierach reported German workers showed an ulcer rate that was eight times as high for rotating than for fixed shift workers.[8] Another study reported the same rate to be four times as high. Thiis-Evensen found the incidence of ulcers was about twice as high for shift workers as for day workers.[9] In a careful review of research in the area this same researcher points out that comparisons of ulcer rates of shift and day workers are of little value unless it is possible to specify when the ulcers were contracted. He does, however, conclude that there is probably a relationship between shift work and the recurrence of ulcer symptoms. The demands of shift work may aggravate ulcers already present or speed their reactivation. Thus while these researchers have looked for relationships between the more serious health disorders and shift work, they have not been able to establish causal relationships.

Much less work has been done on the effects of shift work upon family relations and social participation than upon the medical and physiological effects. Different researchers have been concerned with the various obligations the worker has to his family and the community. Some point out that night work disturbs the family life in general; others are more specific about the effects that the absence of the worker in the house in the evening has on the children or on marital sexual relations. Several studies also indicate that evening and night shifts interfere with the worker's participation in voluntary organizations as well as with his contacts with friends and relatives. While in the aggregate there is evidence that shift work has effects upon the worker's family relations, his social participation, and his opportunities for solitary leisure activities, research in this area has been quite fragmentary and unsystematic.

With reference to the shift worker's affective states, the evidence has been even more sparse and contradictory. The worker's satisfaction with shift work is generally unrelated to his other job satisfactions. The single exception is his satisfaction with his wages: the greater his satisfaction with his wages, the more satisfied he is with his shift. The greatest dissatisfaction with shift work has been found among young shift workers and young married workers with small children. Satisfaction with shift work also appears to vary inversely with education and skill level. Some research suggested that shift work leads to the development of negative affective states. However, G. H. Bast has insisted that this hypothesis is inaccurate—that it is only a "stereotype" that shift work disrupts family life and physical health and results in poor psychological health.[10]

A New American Study of the Effects of Shift Work

To get a new, more thorough understanding of the social, psychological, and physical effects of shift work—and especially the interrelationships among these—on a population of American workers, a major study was undertaken as a part of the Industrial Mental Health Program of the Survey Research Center. After an extended search, we were able to locate two groups of continuous process plants within different companies that were unique in that: (1) within the same company plants worked fixed and rotating shifts; (2) within the same company the plants manufactured essentially the same product; and (3) the companies and the unions involved were willing to have the study done. The design of our research called for locating populations of workers that were working day, evening, night, and rotating shifts under the same general job and organizational conditions so that we could investigate the effects of shift and nonshift work schedules, and different types of shift work schedules, such as fixed and rotating. The study plan for which we settled finally allowed us to study the following work schedules: fixed day shift, fixed evening shift, fixed night shift, and weekly rotation of shifts. These continuous process plants were in the east-central part of the United States, in areas that ranged from almost rural to a large metropolitan center. Male shift workers and the wives of married workers were included in the study. Respondents were selected from lists of workers provided by the company or the union. Data were collected in 1960 by comprehensive paper-and-pencil questionnaires and interviews from 1,045 blue-collar workers and 661 of their wives.

To explore the effects of different shift patterns on family and social life, questions were asked about how the work schedule affected the worker's opportunity to fulfill different aspects of requirements of his role as husband, father, relative, friend, and citizen compared with the difficulty he would experience if he were working steady days. As might be expected, in the aggregate the findings indicated that the amount of difficulty reported was related to the degree to which there was conflict between the time that an activity usually occurs and the schedule of working hours. A few examples may be helpful. The afternoon shift worker, who is absent from home in the late afternoon and evening hours, generally reported the greatest difficulty in the role behaviors associated with early evening. These workers had the greatest difficulty in spending time with their children and doing things with them, in teaching their children skills, and in providing their wives with companionship, and diversion and relaxation from their household duties. Rotating shift workers scored about the same on these roles as the evening workers, for they experienced these problems one-third of the time. Night shift workers reported much more difficulty than afternoon shift workers in meeting those aspects of their family roles that are usually associated with the later evening hours: sexual relations and protection of the wife from harm. In short, there was a good deal of evidence that evening, night, and rotating shift work creates difficulties for all shift workers in the execution of their family responsibilities.

The effects of these difficulties on the marriage relationship were looked into carefully. It was found that working shifts was inversely related to the functional integration—the adequacy of coordination and problem-solving—in the family. Moreover, because the functional integration of the shift working family was less adequate, the amount of strain and tension found in this type of family was higher. Working shifts did not seem to affect the amount of marital happiness reported by the partners.

With reference to social activities, shift work did not seem to interfere with informal social life—visiting with friends and relatives. The only family social activity that was more difficult for the shift worker was attending weddings and related formal activities which were temporarily inflexible. The findings on frequency of contact also revealed no consistent differences between the day shift and the other shifts. One clear finding was that the rotating shift worker reported far fewer friends than either day workers or other shift workers.

In the area of participation in the activities of voluntary associations, shift work also had an effect. Shift workers belonged to fewer organizations than did day workers. If the shift worker did belong to organizations, he was still less likely than the day workers to be an officer or hold a committee assignment.

Three criteria of the worker's psychological reactions to shift work were used in this study: self-esteem, anxiety, and conflict-pressure.[11] None of these measures was found to be directly related to the worker's shift. To determine how the worker perceived his work schedule—the extent to which his shift, compared to the work of the steady day worker, facilitated or interfered with his various role behaviors and activities—a measure of the total interference felt by the worker across all of his role behaviors was constructed. This measure of perceived interference was found to be related to different shifts, and it was this measure that related to our criteria of psychological health. The greater the interference felt by the worker across all of his roles and activities, the lower his self-esteem, and the higher his anxiety and conflict pressure. Difficulties in the roles of father and husband or in engaging in social activities or hobbies were significantly related to the criteria of psychological health. However, difficulties in performance of roles as a member of voluntary associations were not related to psychological health. More complex analyses suggest that these findings could not be attributed to the neuroticism of the worker: The basic relationship between level of difficulty and the measures of psychological reactions was greater for those workers who were low on our measure of neuroticism. On the whole, the personality attributes of the worker appeared to be less important to understanding the relationship between perceived role difficulty and self-esteem, anxiety, and conflict pressure than the interference felt by his wife and her willingness and ability to adjust to his working hours.

The physical effects of shift work on the shift worker were looked into in this new study by asking the men to report on their health and sense of well-being. As in previous studies it was found that reported difficulties with time-oriented body functions—sleeping, eating, and bowel habits—were related to the shift of the worker. More workers on the steady night and rotating shifts reported that they had difficulty in adjusting these body functions to the needs of their shift. However, the more serious health complaints—for example, ulcers—were found to be highest among the day and afternoon shift workers. It appeared that the shift worker who had experienced the most serious physical problems had been able to obtain a transfer to the day shift. This could not be definitely established because the tracing of an ailment to its date of onset and the shift on which the worker was at the time was found to be virtually impossible within the design of this study.

To extend the analysis a little further for subsequent researchers, two measures of complaints about the functions of time-oriented body functions were constructed and related to the more serious health complaints. One measured the general level of complaints among all workers in terms of the extent to which they felt fatigued, had trouble sleeping, appetite problems, and bowel problems. The second—the reported rate of body adjustment—measured the ability of rotating shift workers to adjust their eating, sleeping, and bowel habits to their changing shift schedule. Both of these measures were found to be related to the measures of health of the workers. The more difficulty the workers reported on one or both of these measures, the poorer was their general health, the higher the level of complaints about upper gastrointestinal difficulties, and the more prevalent the report of ulcers and rheumatoid arthritis.

Worker's complaints about rhythmic functioning were also related to a number of background factors. One of the more significant findings was that the worker's age and length of service on his shift were not related to his complaint level. This finding was a surprise for it might be expected that with the passage of time the worker would become accustomed to his shift.

More complex and integrative analyses suggest that the combined effects of perceived role difficulty and a high level of complaints about the time-oriented body functions were negatively related to psychological health, marital integration and happiness of the worker, and his satisfaction with his shift.[12]

The Relevance of These Findings Concerning Hours of Work

While it is possible to identify the advantages and disadvantages of different schedules of shift work, it is difficult to come out of any careful, extensive investigation of the total impact of shift work on the individual and his family without a feeling of uneasiness. Causal links between shift work and the lack of marital and familial integration, psychological and physical health, and participation in organizational affairs have not been established, but there are enough correlative findings to suggest what might be uncovered if careful, longitudinal studies extended over a number of years were undertaken with the same population of workers, their wives, and their children. And while there is no question but that such studies would indicate that the disadvantages of shift work or of certain shift work patterns—e.g., the fixed rather than rotating schedules—are not large for some populations at certain times in the life cycle of the individual or the family, it is equally clear that shift work has more disadvantages for the majority more often than not. Thus, since it is our best estimate that the economic considerations that lead toward around-the-clock operations will continue, and it is our best estimate that the social, psychological, and physical costs of working shifts are not unimportant, what relevance—if any—should these facts have in discussions concerning the length of the workweek and the work-day? With this question, we are of course moving away from the role of scientist and attempting to think through what implications this body of knowledge about the effects of shift work has on an immediate issue of concern to the nation.

With this caveat, it would not seem inappropriate to state that the facts we have suggest: *That for those who have to adjust their lives and their families to productive processes operating around the clock, fixed shift schedules of six or seven hours a day might be more appropriate than the current pattern of eight hours if these workers could be precluded from taking—or educated about the effects of holding—second jobs.*

This statement raises a series of questions. Let us take them one by one. Why recommend a fixed shift schedule? From our analysis of the aggregative advantages and disadvantages of the different shifts in this study, the fixed shift pattern seems the better arrangement than the weekly rotating shift pattern for the well-being of the worker.[13] The fixed afternoon shift creates the most difficulties for the worker's family and social roles, but the rotating shift is a close second. On the surface, the problem of adjusting the time-oriented body functions seems just as severe for the steady night worker as it does for the rotating shift worker, but the former has the advantage in that he does not have to continue to try and alter his basic body rhythms each week or month. There is another sizable disadvantage to the rotating shift schedule. In the plant with the rotating schedule, the worker either adjusts and continues to adjust to shift work, day in and day out, or he is out of a job. Working a rotating schedule of hours is a condition of employment. The fixed shift schedule allows the worker to request—and the medical director to consider—a transfer to another shift temporarily. Or when the shift worker has enough seniority he can bid for the shift he finds most compatible with his own personal and family needs at that time. N. Kleitman's thorough work on the difficulties that some people experience in altering their sleep-wakefulness cycle would also support our recommendation.[14]

Before considering the question of why we suggest a six- or seven-hour day, what are the cost considerations in the fixed versus rotating shift recommendation? The rotating shift pattern is the predominant one in the continuous process plants today. Careful studies of the economics of different shift patterns indicate that the fixed shift schedule requires fewer men for the same number of jobs. This difference is not, however, very large. But what of the social costs involved in family coordination and strain and of the other hidden costs in what appears to be the worker's less-than-full psychological and physical health? In a society that can solve the multitude of technical problems required to place satellites in orbit around the earth and to develop telemetering instruments capable of monitoring the weather as it develops, it is significant that we still do not have the capacity to translate what economists have so long called "social costs" into the dollars-and-cents language of "economic costs."

Why a six- or seven-hour day? A six-hour shift from midnight to morning is a long day psychologically and physically, especially if the body rhythms have not been converted to that span of hours as a work period. A six-hour shift in the evening is a long day sociologically if the man has affiliative needs that are best met by associating with his family, his friends, and by being in organization activities. With only a six-hour day—and especially with the right positioning of the starting times of shifts—the father of children of school age can have time with them regularly to help in the direction of their growth. Whether five or six of these six- or seven-hour days should be put together to constitute a 36-, 30-, 35-hour workweek depends on the larger economic issues of what the economy can afford and whether man wants to take any further gains in additional income or leisure. The aim of this chapter has been to focus on the shift work and its consequences.

Now why the prescription against the second job? There is considerable evidence that in a society like ours where much is invested in creating and shaping consumers' needs and expectations workers with six-hour shifts often take on full- or part-time second jobs.[15] A man may then be working as much as ten to fourteen hours a day. While Paul Mott's findings about the moonlighter (see Chapter 5) suggest that he is so energetic he can maintain two jobs in an attempt to meet high economic aspirations, it is clear that the moonlighter does not do this without cost to his family and his own self-esteem as a father and a husband. Although Mott found that the shift workers in our study who reported holding second jobs indicated membership in more voluntary associations than those who did not, W. L. Ginsberg and R. Bergman state that these men typically have less time, energy, and interest to devote to their union and the union is weaker. Ginsberg and Bergman also state that absenteeism of the rubber workers was markedly higher when the six-hour shift was in effect and dual employment widespread. Mott's data indicate that older workers are much less likely to be holding second jobs; Ginsberg and Bergman report that the older, more highly paid, and skilled workers were more in favor of the shorter workday, feeling that six hours at a fast pace was enough. It is essential to note that the experience of the rubber industry with the six-hour, six-day schedule underscores the point that *both* management and the workers need to understand more about the long-range social, psychological, and physical effects of shift work. Before our society with its demand to consume can move toward a shorter workday or workweek, more evidence about the effects of working the odd shifts will need to be accumulated and given to the public, or scheduling shorter shifts may simply result in the taking of more second jobs.

Summary

Shift work is a concomitant of an increasingly industrial and scientific society. Recent and continuing technological changes in plant and office indicate that shift work will continue to be a requirement for many workers and their families. Studies of the effects of shift work in Europe and the United States suggest that the social, psychological, and physical costs of working shifts are not unimportant. It appears that some of these disadvantages could be materially reduced by having those who have to man productive processes operating around the clock work a fixed shift work schedule with a shorter day.

Notes

1. Donald N. Michael, *Cybernation: The Silent Conquest,* Santa Barbara, Calif., Center for the Study of Democratic Institutions, 1962.

2. P. E. Mott, F. C. Mann, Q. McLoughlin, and D. Warwick, *Shift Work: Social, Psychological and Physical Consequences,* Ann Arbor, Mich., The University of Michigan Press, 1965.

3. F. C. Mann, "Psychological and Organizational Impacts," in J. T. Dunlop, ed., *Automation and Technological Change,* Englewood Cliffs, N.J., Prentice-Hall, Inc., 1962, pp. 43–65.

4. Clyde E. Dankert, "Shorter Hours and Multiple Shifts: A Future Pattern?" *Personnel,* 1959, XXXVI, pp. 61–69.

5. A more thorough review of this literature can be found in the first chapter of P. E. Mott, *et al., op. cit.*

6. E. Thiis-Evensen, "Shift Work and Health," *Industrial Medicine,* XXVII (1958), XXVII, pp. 493–497.

7. V. Bjerner, A. Holm, and A. Swenssen, *Om Nott—Och Shiftavhete,* Stockhold, Statnes Offenttiga Utredningar 51, 1948.

8. A. Pierach, "Nachtarbeit und Schichtweschsel Beim Gesunden und Kranken Measchen," *Acta Medica Scandinavica,* 1955, Supp. 307, pp. 159–166.

9. E. Thiis-Evensen, *op. cit.*

10. G. H. Bast, *Ploegenarbeid in de Industry,* Arnheim, Contractgroepveering Productivitect Van Loghum Staterus, 1960.

11. The latter two are measures of emotional or affective states: anxiety being a feeling of uneasiness, worry, and of imminent but uncertain, unpleasant experiences; and conflict-pressure being a feeling of tension due to the lack of satisfaction of basic needs. See R. B. Cattell and I. H. Scheier, *The Meaning*

and Measurement of Neuroticism and Anxiety, New York, The Ronald Press, 1961.

12. This has been a very brief summary of the findings from this new study. The reader concerned with this problem will want to read the full volume to obtain the whole story.

13. See section entitled "The Advantages and Disadvantages of Each Shift," in Chap. 8 of P. E. Mott, *et al., op. cit.*

14. N. Kleitman, "The Sleep-Wakefulness Cycle of Submarine Personnel," in *Human Factors in Underseas Warfare,* Washington, D.C., National Research Council, 1949.

15. W. L. Ginsberg and R. Bergman, "Workers Attitudes toward Shorter Hours," *Monthly Labor Review,* LXXIX, No. 11 (November 1956), pp. 1268–1270.

8. Automation, Rationalization, and Urbanization: Hours of Work in the Office

DEAN F. BERRY

Department of Industry
Wharton School of Finance and Commerce
University of Pennsylvania

Institutional lags (in which Parkinson created so much delight) are as prevalent in interest-preserving research associations as in governmental establishments. It is not jarring to one's professional equilibrium to find that after the nation's human resource mix changed in the mid-fifties to a predominantly white-collar input, the annual IRRA volume a decade later would concern itself primarily with blue-collar unionized occupations. Of more concern is the discovery, in 1963, by the President's Committee to Appraise Employment and Unemployment Statistics that: "the Department of Labor should try to gather more information on the hours of work of white collar employees." For in that year white-collar employees outnumbered blue-collar employees by 5.5 million, were, in some basic averages receiving higher pay and benefits, and were predicted to be 50.1 per cent of *all* civilian employment by 1972.[1]

In 1951 the sociological imagination of C. Wright Mills presented to potentially receptive students a vision of such a social-industrial transformation in *White Collar* (New York, Oxford University Press, 1956):

by examining white collar life, it is possible to learn something about what is becoming more typically "American" than the frontier character probably ever was . . . society as a great salesroom, an enormous file, an incorporated brain . . . [yet] for two generations sons and daughters of the poor have looked forward to becoming "mere" clerks. Parents have sacrificed to have even one child finish high school . . . so that he could . . . do something requiring technical skills: hold a white collar job. . . . [pp. xiii-xv]

The decade following *White Collar* bore out the author's assertions. The white-collar group was the fastest growing occupational group in the 1950s and 1960s and is currently predicted (by the BLS) to increase at twice the average *rate* for all fields of work between 1960–1975. The meaning of such a shift in employment has more than sociological importance. The white-collar group throughout its classification now holds more clearly than ever before the highest potential for productivity increases in *both* the goods and services sectors. The white-collar group is frequently cited by labor spokesmen as the major hope for expansion in union membership (and perhaps even influence). It is also the white-collar group that holds the significant absorption potential for the young, the married woman worker, the educated minority group member, and the part-time employee. The preceding groups are the exact classifications of the work force expected to increase by the 1970s. Whether these groups will in fact be employed in the numbers predicted is, on both the demand and supply side, influenced by the hours of work of the clerical and kindred occupations.

Clerical Workers[2]

An increasing number of the large group (15 per cent of the employed) of clerical workers are working fewer than 40 hours, less are working 40 hours, and there is a 10 per cent drop over the decade of those working more than 40 hours. Such a trend reflects a decline in over-all scheduled hours of work, but the statistics also reflect an increased utilization of less than full-time employees and a marked postwar reduction in scheduled hours of work in the non-manufacturing industries not covered by FLSA. The important aspects of clerical work that lead to a distinct reduction in weekly hours of work are:

1. Standard clerical workweeks of less than 40 hours in manufacturing that are increasing in number

2. The clerical workers (the largest proportion of those 6 per cent of the employed in the 35–39 hours category) who are represented more than proportionately in the finance, insurance, and real estate industries, particularly those located in the megalopolis regions of the East Coast

3. Certain segments of the retail, service, and trade groups (particularly those under collective bargaining agreements) which, in many instances, have now the 37½-hour week.

The Clerical Work Force and Its Problem

The clerical component of the white-collar group finds its workweek decreasing while its numbers are expanding. And, along with rising capital-to-worker ratios in the office, we are informed that the cost of today's average business letter (250 words) is now $2.32 as compared with $1.17 in 1953 and $1.97 in 1962.[3] Simultaneously, NPA and BLS projections reveal a large potential expansion of clerical opportunities. Various union groups are interested in the supply side of such projections in the hope that clerical work-force expansions could absorb "silent firings" and a portion of the presently unemployed. Economists and other social scientists are hopeful that clerical expansion will provide employment for minority groups, the young, the part-time workers, and even create opportunities for married women. It is my contention that the likelihood of such opportunities on *both* the demand and supply side are doubtful for a variety of socio-technical reasons. In sum, the mechanization of service and administrative tasks (with attendant changes in job requirements and work patterns) and demographic shifts of potential white-collar employees and employers are acting to contract the growth of work opportunities for the clerical work force. To explore this position, let us first look at a summary of some pertinent characteristics of the clerical work force.

1. *Age—Sex:* Two-thirds female, concentrated in the under 25 and over 45 age group. Males are predominantly over 45 and in the high skill jobs.

2. *Job stability:* Clerical women in the service-trade-finance industries (such industries being primarily in urban locations) have short job tenures (2½ years, on the average). Their jobs are low in skill, pay, and benefits. Clerical jobs in the manufacturing sector appear, however, to experience less turnover (20 per cent as compared to 30 per cent in service-financial), have lower separation rates, and in their turnover and separation cases a higher proportion leaves to take another job (53 per cent as compared to 26 per cent in the service-financial sector).[4]

3. *Distribution:* While clerical workers make up a fairly standard percentage of occupational employment by geographic region, several factors must be noted. The largest employment gains for clericals in the future will come from the financial-insurance-real estate-trade-and-service sectors. These businesses are, by and large, centrally located in urban areas. Manufacturing businesses are moving to suburban and rural locations.

4. *Education and skills:* The bulk of the clerical and kindred jobs (about 70 per cent) seems to be in the low skill grades. The skilled classifications are growing at a much faster rate and high skill office workers tend to work 40-hour weeks while short-hour weeks are concentrated among low skill groups.

Hours Reduction in the Workweek

By 1963 one-third of all clerical workers had a workweek of less than 40 hours. As an occupational classification the clerical grouping has fewer scheduled workweeks of over 40 hours than any other classification. The Metropolitan Occupational Pay Surveys of the BLS reveal further where these short workweeks are concentrated. While 40 per cent of all office workers in metropolitan areas work less than 40 hours, 60 per cent of the clerical office workers in the Northeast are scheduled for less than 40 hours. Countrywide, each of the four regions shows at least one-sixth of the clerical office workers in their metropolitan areas to have workweeks of less than 40 hours. For the nation as a whole, 87 per cent of all clerical and office workers actually work 40 hours or less, up 10 per cent from 1952. By region, scheduled hours of less than 40 cover 62 per cent of Northeast office employees but only 25 per cent or less of the office workers in the South, North Central, and West. Clerical and office workers covered by (or strongly tied to) collective bargaining agreements show the same trend, as evidenced by these selected New York metropolitan settlements over the past few years.

1. The New York Council of Wholesale Meat Dealers, Inc. (*et al.*) in bargaining with the Amalgamated Meat Cutters and Butcher Workmen reduced the office workweek from 40 to 35 hours, effective January 1961.

2. Several city department stores (Bloomingdale's, Macy's, and Gimbel's) in bargaining with District 65 of the Retail, Wholesale and Department Store Union agreed to reduce workweeks from 40 hours to 37½ hours for nine months of the year (excluding the three-month Christmas season) starting in 1963–1964.

It appears reasonable to conclude that clerical and office workers are working shorter hours, that the trend has been going on over the past decade, and that the concentration of the short workweek activity is a metropolitan trend, particularly in the service sector. However, the trend is moving to the manufacturing sector as well.

Hours Reduction: Workyear and Worklife

An alternative method (to the scheduled length of the workweek) of regarding an hours of work question is to measure hours per year

TABLE 1.   TREND OF SCHEDULED WEEKLY HOURS, 18 METROPOLITAN
AREAS, 1952–1953 AND 1961–1962ª

| Scheduled Hours of Office Workers | Per Cent of Workers in | | | |
| | All Industries | | Manufacturing | |
	1952–1953	1961–1962	1952–1953	1961–1964
Less than 40 hours	44	47	27	33
40 hours	53	53	70	66
Over 40 hours	3	1	3	1
All hours	100	100	100	100

SOURCE: Bureau of Labor Statistics, "Occupational Wage Surveys."
ª Because of rounding, sums of individual percentages may not equal totals.

or per worker life cycle. Under present fringe benefit considerations, then, it is necessary to look at paid-for days for which time is not worked; namely, paid holidays, paid vacations, early retirement with pension benefits, and paid-for sabbaticals. To the extent that sick days, or time off for personal reasons, and leaves of absence are paid for these items also become relevant.

Paid Vacations and Holidays

While paid vacations for office workers have been quite common for many years, it has been during the last quarter of a century that such vacations have become almost universal. In addition to the "horizontal" growth in vacations, there has been a "vertical" expansion as well: Vacation rights have been greatly liberalized. For example, only 22 per cent of the office workers in metropolitan areas in 1952–1953 were granted vacations of three weeks or more after ten years' service, but by 1962–1963 the figure stood at 52 per cent. It should be noted, though, that the high attrition and turnover ratios of clerical workers considerably dampen the economic effect of liberalized vacations.

Paralleling the increased liberalization of vacation benefits in the office over the past ten years has been the extension of paid holidays. As with paid vacations, office workers have received, and continue to receive, somewhat better treatment than plant workers.[5] Ninety-eight per cent of office workers in both the 1952–1953 and 1962–1963 periods received six days or more. The percentages for plant workers were 86 and 92, respectively. While the average number of holidays for office workers is eight, over one-half of these workers in the finance industry receive nine or more and over one-third, eleven or more. For obvious selling-day reasons, retail trade provides the fewest holidays; and manufacturing lags behind services. An interesting development has been the increase in the practice of "bunching" holidays together or around weekends (for instance, the granting of a Friday holiday following Thanksgiving).

Sick Leaves, Pensions, and Sabbaticals

Although information about these factors is scanty, their future economic effect may be large. For example, as will be established later, automation increases the physical workload of office workers and tends to upgrade the young and trainable males. Also many debilitating illnesses (heart disease, ulcers, and others) seem to be more prevalent among office workers, particularly clericals. Insured or paid sick leave and early retirement would have, under these conditions, decided economic effects on hours of work in the life cycle.

Pension plans are widespread among metropolitan office workers covering, in 1960–1961, 77 per cent of those employed. The prevalence of early retirement or vesting provisions is unknown for office workers. Fully compensable sick leave covered 59 per cent of these employees in the same period. Data on all these potentially important variables are largely unobtainable. What information is available is difficult to assess because of the low job stability of the clerical worker.

Summary of Work Hours

One way to summarize the scheduled hours not worked for the clerical workers is to attempt a calculation of increased leisure over a time period. P. Henle has estimated that a full-time employed person in 1960 would have 155 hours per year as increased time available for leisure over a similar employee in 1940.[6]

For an office worker in an Eastern financial office the BLS states that if the hours paid for is 100 per cent, paid-for hours not worked are distributed as follows: 3.5 per cent in vacations, 2.9 per cent in holidays, 1.3 per cent in sick leave, and 0.2 per cent in "other," for a total of 7.9 per cent. Using reasonable assumptions from data developed thus far, the *increase* in time not worked but paid for (for a clerical located in the East, 1940–1963) would look like this:

		Hours Per Year *Per Full-time* *Employed Clerical*
1.	3 hours less in the workweek	150
2.	7 days more paid vacation	56
3.	6 days more paid holidays	48
4.	2 days more in paid sick leave	16
	Total	270
		(Hours gained, 1940–1963)

The data developed to this point would seem to support this admittedly broad estimation. If even approximately accurate, however, the 270 hours amount to almost seven average workweeks. Have the office occupations improved productivity to this degree?

Productivity estimates have been somewhat meaningless for the office because possible office efficiency usually appears to be sacrificed for improvements in quality or in the expansion of services. A more complete knowledge of the office work situation is basic to any estimates of probable productivity trends now or in the future. In addition, insights into the on-the-job factors affecting clerical work provide some leverage for questioning the projections of office work-force growth. It is the main contention of this chapter that "clerical and kindred" work-force extrapolations are unrealistic. It seems doubtful that the clerical employment sector is going to provide the kinds of job opportunities mentioned earlier due, in large part, to certain qualitative job characteristics.

Qualitative influences on Office Work

As scientific management rationalized the assembly line, modern
office management is rationalizing office work. Issues of *Office, Office
Management,* and similar journals contain spates of articles on such
topics as "time study," "environetics," and "work flow."

Automation

The first big office installation of a computer took place in the
insurance industry in 1953. We are now in the second decade of
office automation. Today a broadly diversified number of smaller-
slower units (capable of system integration) offered at lower prices
can do an increased number of tasks and thereby reach a greater
share of office situations. For example, in 1960 Diebold and Associates were able to develop the data in Table 2. Certainly the small-
medium systems have expanded since then as the current rate of
production is about 10,000 units per year.

Direct Effects of Office Automation

There are enough good studies (both domestic and foreign) to
enable generalizations about the direct effects of office automation.[7]

1. *Job content.* Certain evidence suggests that the tempo of job
content change is rising, particularly with the addition of office automation.[8] The old image of stability in white-collar job content,
typified by the eye-shaded bookkeeper, is now an anachronism.
Actually, under automation skill requirements rise relatively slowly
as the low skill people need even less skill and programming and
processing upgrade the already highly skilled. It is well to point
out that in these automation studies the bulk of the job assignments
was from routine jobs to automated routine jobs for younger, less
stable employees. The older employees were generally not promoted
to new positions nor were they selected for training. Therefore, in
addition to concern about total clerical employment, it appears

TABLE 2. ELECTRONIC DATA-PROCESSING APPLICATIONS IN THE
UNITED STATES ECONOMY AS A PERCENTAGE OF TOTAL
DATA-PROCESSING MARKET, 1960[a]

Economic Sector	Small-Medium Systems	Large Systems
Agriculture	.4	–
Mining	.7	–
Contract construction	1.0	–
Manufacturing	*50.1*	*33.4*
Food-Textile	11.6	2.2
Process industry (including metals)	14.7	10.4
Machinery	12.4	9.5
Transportation	5.9	8.6
Other	5.5	2.7
Wholesale and retail trade	10.7	7.4
Finance, insurance, and real estate	10.8	13.9
Transportation	9.0	8.4
Communication and public utilities	2.8	6.8
Services	2.8	5.5
Government	*11.7*	*24.6*
Federal	8.3	22.3
State and local	3.4	2.3
Total	100.0	100.0

[a] Data developed by John Diebold and Associates, Inc.

reasonable to conclude that present, high turnover rates will stay high or even increase as the majority of clerical employees who are unfavorably affected by automation quit, retire, or take leaves of absence, thus further reducing total clerical hours of work.

2. *Job displacement and turnover*. Little immediate displacement appears to take place under automation. Most persons from eliminated jobs are apparently offered opportunities in other company areas that are expanded due to the effects of the computer. For example, the BLS estimates that the average computer abolishes

about thirty-five clerical jobs. If, as cited above, 10,000 automated units per year are produced, 350,000 clerical jobs per year would be eliminated; but the employees may remain. However, if yearly clerical turnover approaches 25 per cent (of a 10-thousand group), nearly 2.5 thousand clericals would leave their present job in that period. While attrition and turnover can conceal job displacement and relocation, turnover appears to be more a result of "femaleness" than automation. The work attitudes and characteristics of women *qua* women influence clerical job patterns, change, and job costs. Some of these influences are imposed restrictions (hours per day, hazardous surroundings, prohibited night work, physical effort). Others have to do with female job characteristics in view of changing opportunities or circumstances. Facing situations where they work out of necessity and do not advance in a firm, it would seem logical that many married women would pay little attention to qualitative job considerations (until once on the job) and would then have little commitment to a firm. Such an outlook would be reinforced by the single woman's intention not to remain at all.

Questions of Interpretation

It is necessary to call attention to one key assumption about automation that is, unfortunately, frequently taken for granted. Automation in an office may be exploited along *three* paths: (1) expanding outside services (e.g., a bank providing payroll reconciliation for its noncomputerized industrial customers at a small cost); (2) expanding internal services (e.g., providing machine load scheduling on computer time not used for accounting office work such as billing); (3) and/or internal reduction of costs. Recent unpublished studies by Boris Yavitz at Columbia indicate that there are no clear ways of predicting which paths are chosen. Most "scare" journalism assumes the path of internal cost reduction and hence layoffs. While conclusions on exploitation paths are strongly influenced by the nature of the industry, it is obvious that service-oriented industries have all three paths as choices and these same industries are predicted to have the greatest increase in clerical employment. The paths chosen to exploit this office technology will be the deciding force in job creation or destruction. At this writing the direction of office technology exploitation is unclear, but for many reasons (e.g., regulatory and legal) it does not seem plausible for the path to continue to be that of providing increased service.

Unionization of Clericals

Typical arguments for unionization possibilities rest on the increasing similarity of rationalized white-collar jobs with mechanized and automated blue-collar jobs. Such studies generally ignore the turnover at one end and the creation of the new elite of programmers, etc., at the other.[9] Lower skill jobs and downgraded jobs tend to turn over faster for the many reasons unrelated to job satisfaction explained previously. Such experience would counter the union notion that after automation employees are either frozen at occupational levels or routinized thereby creating a potential for organization. On the other hand, as skills upgrade in the office, and the studies cited indicate that they do because of automation and rationalization, the office work force becomes upgraded in status and education. Office workers with higher education, status, and skills tend to have greater identification with management.[10] While office-worker values do not seem to be as white-collar oriented as was once thought, the empirical study that concluded: "identification with management is not as close, and the dissociation from labor not as great as the stereotype has traditionally implied" also noted that "those persons with a longer office work history . . . [are] characterized by negative attitudes toward all types of workers."[11]

The main area for office employee unionization opportunities is in selected urban areas and in selected industries that already have short hours. In these industries office unionization would seem to be waiting for a breakthrough in the professional-technical ranks.

Consequences of Automation, Rationalization, and Urbanization

Skills, Health, and Employment Policies

While it is impossible to conclude whether the nature of the job has attracted less physically healthy employees than desirable, or whether the job influences health, recent evidence indicates that office health lags behind both plant health and executive health.[12] Several studies show that heart disease is greater (in one study twice as great) for office and clerical workers than for executives, and is highest for clericals, considering all industrial groupings of equivalent ages. Other studies indicate like trends for peptic ulcers and diabetes. It is significant that emotional stress and lack of physical activity are of etiological importance in all these diseases.

As a result of differing physical and intellectual demands, office employment policies are changing. Skills required for new hires are moving upward. Standard qualifications for a large share of work in automated office situations are a high school degree with mathematical aptitude and the ability and capacity for training. Also preferred are workers who are flexible, mobile, and responsive to change. The extreme office elites of programmers and data processors are composed primarily of young, well educated *men* who can meet the physical and intellectual demands. This group would have promotion potential (and thereby different values) because requisite managerial skills are also changing radically with a decided emphasis on logical analysis and planning for automated systems.[13]

Silent Firings

Recent estimates conclude that the period of time from the design of an automated office work flow to its eventual "debugged" operation is minimally three years. Any substantial changes in employment will not show up for at least that long, particularly because many firms run "parallel systems" until the automated line runs efficiently.

Office computer sales have had their biggest volume in the period 1960–1963. It is of more than passing interest to note the *rate* of increase in clerical employment over the past thirteen years. The growth rate was lower in 1962 than in the decade of the fifties and for 1963 it was down appreciably.

TABLE 3. GROWTH RATE OF WHITE-COLLAR OCCUPATION

	Average Gain *1959–1960*	*Gain* *1962*	*Gain* *1963*
All white collar	2.81%	2.6%	0.9%
Professional, technical	6.66	4.4	2.7
Clerical	2.89	2.4	1.6

SOURCE: *Wall Street Journal*, CLXIII, No. 89 (May 5, 1964).

The 1962–1963 employment growth in the clerical occupations was only 280,000 at a time when total nonfarm employment rose by 1.4 million. W. S. Buckingham has pointed out that the rate of increase in the number of clerical employees in companies installing automated processing equipment is only half the increase in nonautomated companies.[14]

I. R. Hoos points out that office automation's effect on employment may take several years to work out.[15] She indicates that in geographically dispersed and decentralized companies centralization starts occurring two to three years after office automation. At that time branch offices or installations must lay off, downgrade, or not promote. The growth in the white-collar work force in the office must come, then, from other than the large Eastern finance, real estate, and insurance offices.

Part-Timers, Married Women, and Minority Groups

It has been suggested that the new career orientation of women, upward-shifting family income aspiration levels, and the rise of the permanent part-time worker may offset high clerical turnover and provide the needed higher level of skills for automated offices. Also it has been observed that the new, and rising, part-time work force could absorb some of the predicted expansion in the clerical and office field, particularly if automated offices go to shift schedules, and thereby increase employment and perhaps total hours of clerical workers by reducing the average hours of work. Such proposals do not seem persuasive in light of the following facts:

1. While the demand is increasing for part-time people (although still considerably below the supply) the need comes largely from the service sector. A service business faced with changing shopping habits resulting from urbanization finds need for part-timers to handle fluctuating peak-and-valley customer demands and lengthened store hours and days. Considering the extension of FLSA regulations on overtime pay and the lowered hourly rates and fringe benefit costs for part-timers, service industries are employing more part-time help. But the service sector has traditionally recruited outside the labor force (teenagers, married housewives, and retirees), and much of the work is only for a few hours per week.

2. As offices become more automated the necessity for maintaining a continuous, integrated work flow is increased. Much of the automated office services, particularly in the growing manufacturing sector, are "real-time" data operations which are only useful when the company is operating; not, for example, during a night shift. Shorter work hours, particularly on shifts, increase the complexity of scheduling and decrease the flexibility of planning. More total workers would probably be preferred for an equivalent full-time, day operation.

3. There are severe temporal consequences for the shift worker in terms of the ways in which he cannot, and does not, use leisure (e.g., he does not participate in community affairs, church, social organizations, or visit with friends and relatives, etc.).[16] Women's work-home schedules would be difficult to adjust to other than day employment. The workweek for married women with children who work full time (and travel to and from work) is still long. H. Wilensky estimates

80 hours.[17] A half-time job still creates long hours and burdens for shopping and other outside-the-home family duties.

4. The much heralded return to the permanent work force of married women seems to be feminist nostalgia, at least until age 40–45, and then for more professionally inclined women.[18] A recent study concluded that for a woman to perform in both traditional home and career roles, she needed: (a) a positive attitude of her husband toward her employment, (b) a previous occupation which required training or educational achievement, (c) a previous work experience *after* marriage, (d) her children to be of school age, and (e) her husband to accept some obligation for child care and household chores.[19] Most American women, 65 per cent, do not work outside the home. Those that do are largely in blue-collar or low skill clerical or service jobs. The recent increases in commutation time and lack of adequate child-care centers (or like institutional arrangements) should continue to reinforce the present pattern of women working early or late in their life cycles and not increase their participation rate in the full-time labor force substantially over the foreseeable future.

Color Barriers

The Equal Employment Opportunity Committee (a Presidential committee to enforce executive orders on discrimination) recently released a statistical study of 4,160 companies. The report concentrated on the white-collar jobs in which Negroes have made little penetration. From 1962–1963 the percentage of Negroes employed by the companies increased from 1.2 to 1.3 per cent. The gain in Negro white-collar employment was largest in the large, eastern, industrialized cities. But of the 4,160 companies studied, 3,700 showed no change in Negro employment, 327 reported decreases, and the remainder showed increases. The executive director of the committee remarked that the share of employment by minorities still "can be measured by fractions."[20] The increasing educational requirements for office work and the apparent lack of business and union attitudinal change do not create the promise of employment gains in clerical occupations for minority groups.

Conclusions

The largely qualitative analysis engaged in here leads to different conclusions that those of the labor economist and statistician. It seems unlikely that the clerical labor force will continue to grow at the previous high rates and should taper off drastically in the next few years. The only substantial expansion will come from additional demand for new office work and that only in service industries in urban areas. The age-sex distribution of newly automated clerical workers will shift toward a larger number of males, with two consequences: (1) Hours of work will not continue to decline, stabilizing somewhere between 37–40 hours per week; (2) the participation rate for nonwhite clericals will not expand as rapidly as predicted. Increasingly, automated offices will have a work flow unsuited to part-time help, geared more to the general operating hours of the firm. High turnover at lower levels will be counteracted by advanced training techniques for these rationalized jobs. Unionization of office work does not seem probable in any large, countrywide degree. In the vulnerable large, Eastern automated offices, what unionization might occur should only solidify present low scheduled hours.

Due to the complexity of work scheduling, offices will prefer longer vacations and more holidays rather than shorter scheduled weekly hours. Pay scales will probably grow faster than presently (with the current unfilled demand for skilled office workers), thereby forcing management to devote more managerial efforts to increase office productivity. The economic areas that will experience increases in clerical employment (but probably no major changes below a 40-hour week because of possible part-time help in the suburbs) are: (1) the suburbs, where more manufacturing offices are moving, and (2) the suburban service and distribution sector where more white-collar workers will be needed on odd-hour bases. An evaluation of these forces waits upon basic data collection.

Work in the office will become physically and intellectually demanding for young males and the office will see a greater number of specialists that are neither managers nor professionals, necessitating different personnel policies than now prevail. Finally, the task of administering the change in the office, the greatly increased capital and indirect labor costs, and the possibility of organizing drives will be the taxing job of the managers, who are in critically short supply and already work long hours.

Notes

1. All data in this chapter are from the Bureau of Labor Statistics unless specifically noted otherwise. Much of the BLS data, as well as official departmental positions, were taken from Part 1 of *Hours of Work,* Ewan Clague's testimony before the Select Subcommittee on Labor, House of Representatives, 88th Cong., 1st Sess., 1964.

2. The Census Bureau and the Bureau of Labor Statistics both use the term "clerical and kindred" to cover an extreme variety of "white-collar" workers. "Kindred" includes mail carriers, telegraphers, and switchboard operators. Clerical workers themselves include postal clerks, cashiers in restaurants and supermarkets, and clerical workers in warehouses. The generalizations offered in this chapter will concentrate on the clerical office worker as that designation covers the majority of this whole occupational category.

3. *Industrial Relations News,* March 14, 1964, Dartnell Corporation, Chicago.

4. "Employee Turnover," *Advanced Management-Office Executive,* August 1963, pp. 12–15.

5. This is probably due to the fact that the largest proportion of clerical and office workers work for large corporations.

6. P. Henle, "Recent Growth of Paid Leisure for U. S. Workers," *Monthly Labor Review,* LXXXV, No. 3 (March 1962), p. 256.

7. See for example, "Impact of Automation," U. S. Bureau of Labor Statistics *Bulletin* No. 1287; "Adjustments to the Introduction of Office Automation," *Bulletin* No. 1276; "Personnel Administration and Office Automation," *ILR,* VIII, No. 3, 1962; I. R. Hoos, *Automation in the Office,* Public Affairs Press, Washington, D.C., 1961; E. Hardin, "The Reactions of Employees to Office Automation," *Monthly Labor Review,* LXXXIII, September 1960, and "Computer Automation, Work Environment and Employee Satisfaction," *Industrial and Labor Relations Review,* XIII, July 1960, and "Automation and the Employee," *The Annals,* March 1962, CCCXL, by W. A. Faunce, E. Hardin, and E. H. Jacobsen; and F. C. Mann and L. K. Williams,

"Observations on the Dynamics of a Change to Electronic Data Processing Equipment," *Administrative Science Quarterly*, V, September 1960. See also several foreign studies: E. R. F. W. Crossman, *Automation and Skill*, Her Majesty's Stationery Office, London, 1960, and *Report of the Special Committee of the Senate on Manpower and Employment*, Queen's Printer and Comptroller of Stationery, Ottawa, 1961.

8. "White Collar Restiveness—A Growing Challenge," Industrial Relations Monograph No. 22, New York, Industrial Relations Counselors, Inc., 1963.

9. Two representative studies are: A. A. Blum, "The Prospects for Office Employee Unionization," *16th Annual Proceedings of the IRRA*, 1963, and E. M. Kassalow, "New Union Frontier: White Collar Workers," *The Harvard Business Review*, XL, January–February 1962.

10. Harry R. Dick, "The Office Worker; Attitudes Towards Self, Labor and Management," *Sociological Quarterly*, III, No. 1, 1962.

11. *Ibid.*

12. S. Pell and C. A. D'Alonzo, "Acute Myocardial Infarction in a Large Industrial Population," *Journal of the American Medical Association*, CLXXXV, September 14, 1963. See also R. E. Lee and R. F. Schneider, "Hypertension and Arteriosclerosis in Executive and Nonexecutive Personnel" in the same journal, CLXVII, July 19, 1958.

13. H. S. Leavitt and T. L. Whisler, "Management in the 1980's," *Harvard Business Review*, November–December 1958.

14. W. S. Buckingham, "The Effects of Automation on White Collar Workers," *Employee Relations Bulletin*, Report No. 839, January 2, 1963.

15. I. R. Hoos, "The Impact of Office Automation on Workers," *International Labor Review*, LXXXII, October 1960, and "When the Computer takes over the Office," *Harvard Business Review*, LXXXIII, July–August 1960.

16. See E. H. Blakelock, "A Durkheimian Approach to Some Temporal Problems of Leisure," *Social Problems*, IX, Summer 1961.

17. H. Wilensky, "The Uneven Distribution of Leisure; the Impact of Economic Growth on Free Time," *Social Problems*, IX (Summer 1961), pp. 32–56.

18. See, for example, "Women in America," *Daedalus*, XCIII, No. 2, Spring 1964, and *The Feminine Mystique* by Betty Frieden, New York, W. W. Norton, 1963.

19. M. W. Weil, "An Analysis of the Factors Influencing Married Women's Actual or Planned Work Participation," *American Sociological Review*, XXVI, No. 1, February 1961.

20. J. D. Pomfret, *New York Times*, July 8, 1964.

9. Hours and Output*

DAVID G. BROWN

Department of Economics
University of North Carolina

The desirability and feasibility of shorter workweeks are intimately related to the effects of shorter hours upon output. To the extent that output and hours of work are negatively related, all parties gain by shorter hours. When hours are reduced employees enjoy higher real incomes and more leisure hours, employers receive higher real incomes, and the total output level of the economy is higher. If, on the other hand, hours of work and output are positively related such that a reduction in the workweek causes a reduction in output, movement to shorter hours means more leisure time but less output. Leisure time is increased at the sacrifice of real income. In this chapter an attempt is made to define the circumstances under which hours reduction requires the sacrifice of real income and the extent of this sacrifice. Specifically, the analysis is directed toward the following questions: what length workweek yields the largest output? In terms of output sacrifice, what is the opportunity cost of reducing the workweek?

* I am indebted to Hugh High, the University of North Carolina Business Foundation, and the University of North Carolina Computation Center for assistance in the preparation of this chapter.

Herein "output" shall mean the "total output of the relevant economic unit": total output of a man, of an industry, or of the economy. For the purpose of measuring economic well-being, the alternative interpretation of "output," output per man-hour, is not appropriate. Output per man-hour is a measure of the efficiency of production, not the level. Though total output reflects changes in output per man-hour, the reverse is not true.

Empirical Evidence

A number of studies of the "before and after" variety have been conducted to determine the nature of the relationship between hours and output. In different plants output is noted before and after a change in hours. The primary limitation of these studies is an understandable failure to hold "other things constant." Scheduled hours of work in most firms are changed infrequently. The circumstances that are of sufficient importance to cause a change in work hours also cause other changes so that isolating the effects of the hours change is virtually impossible. For example, when hours are increased in wartime to mitigate critical scarcities, the work force is often bombarded with new patriotic propaganda and, perhaps, new equipment. Often the number of shifts is increased and many new workers are hired. Sometimes workers are switched from day work to piece rates. Even when concomitant changes are not made simultaneous with changes in hours, since some of the effects of the hours change cannot be evaluated until about a year has elapsed, other things are almost certain not to remain equal during the entire study period.

Case Studies

Having issued the caveat it is still relevant to look at the studies, for they represent the most precise empirical data available on the hours-output relationship. Table 1 presents, in summary form, some of the results of these studies. Here, 1,233 different observations are reported: 940 from the National Industrial Conference Board's mail survey of employers in five industries which had recently reduced

TABLE 1. SUMMARY OF CASE STUDIES[a]

Group	Number of Case Studies	Shorter Hours Result in More Or the Same Output	Longer Hours Result in More Output
By longest workweek (original hours for decreases and new hours for increases):[b]			
More than 60 hours	238 (85)	47% (61%)	53% (39%)
52–60 hours	894 (127)	34% (30%)	66% (70%)
Less than 52 hours	91 (81)	18% (12%)	82% (88%)
By direction of change:[b]			
Hours increased	[e] (124)	[e] (8%)	[e] (92%)
Hours decreased	[e] (169)	[e] (52%)	[e] (48%)
By extent of change in hours:[b]			
More than 15%	[e] (152)	[e] (16%)	[e] (84%)
Less than 15%	[e] (133)	[e] (48%)	[e] (52%)
By method of payment:[e]			
Piece work	325 (138)	33% (17%)	67% (83%)
Time work	261 (48)	23% (23%)	77% (77%)
By type of work:[d]			
Heavy	[e] (33)	[e] (27%)	[e] (73%)
Medium and light	[e] (174)	[e] (24%)	[e] (76%)
By behavior of wage rate:[d]			
Rate increased as hours decreased	280 ([f])	35% ([f])	65% ([f])
Rate remained the same as hours decreased	114 ([f])	33% ([f])	67% ([f])
By sex:[d]			
Male workers	[e] (120)	[e] (25%)	[e] (75%)
Female workers	[e] (76)	[e] (26%)	[e] (74%)

SOURCE: Derived from data contained in the following: H. M. Vernon, *Industrial Fatigue and Efficiency*, London: George Routledge and Sons, Ltd., 1921; U.S. Bureau of Labor Statistics, *Bulletin*, Nos. 791, 791-A, and 917; National Industrial Conference Board, *Research Report*, Nos. 4, 7, 12, 16, 18, 27, and 32; U.S. Bureau of Labor Statistics, *Monthly Labor Review*, Vols. III (pp. 526–543), V (pp. 14–17), XXXII (pp. 1,414–1,421), XLI (pp. 702–705), and LIX (pp. 765–767); S. Wyatt, *A Study of Variations in Output* ("Medical Research Council, Industrial Health Research Board, Emergency Report No. 5"), London: H. M. Stationery Office, 1944; P. Sargant Florence, *Labour*, London: Hutchinson's University Library, 1950, pp. 52–54, and "A Scientific Labour Policy for Industrial Plants," *International Labour Review*, Vol. XLIII (March, 1941), p. 261, and

scheduled workweeks, 158 from the extensive BLS studies during World War II, 93 from the experience in Great Britain during World War I, and 42 from miscellaneous other sources. Because reports by employers on changes in output of an entire plant are probably less reliable than observations of specific work groups by independent observers, in addition to summary data figures are given, in parentheses, which exclude the NICB studies.

If any general conclusions can be drawn from studies which are as diverse in circumstance and methodology as these, it is that the effect of a change in hours upon output varies according to the nature of the change and the conditions under which the change is made. Shorter workweeks are less likely to involve a large sacrifice of output if the following conditions exist:

1. Original work hours are very long. In 47 per cent of the 238 situations where hours were either reduced from above 60 per week or increased to more than 60, total output was no greater for the longer work periods. This contrasts with only 18 per cent of the 91 situations involving workweeks under 52 hours. Omitting the NICB studies, the contrast is even more striking—61 per cent for workweeks over 60 hours long compared with 18 per cent for workweeks under 52 hours. The differences in both sets of data are significant.

2. Work hours are decreased instead of not increased. For ex-

---

The Economics of Fatigue and Unrest, New York: Henry Holt and Co., 1924, pp. 230–232; Marion C. Cahill, *Shorter Hours: A Study of the Movement Since the Civil War,* New York: Columbia University Press, 1932, pp. 226–246; Lujo Brentano, *Hours and Wages in Relation to Production,* London: Swan Sonnenschein and Co., 1894, pp. 30–36; Henry Gavens, *Shorter Hours—How? When?,* Washington: Ransdell, Inc., 1938, pp. 21–22; and Josephine Goldmark, *Fatigue and Efficiency,* New York: Russell Sage Foundation, 1912, pp. 124–170.

a Data in parentheses refer to all studies other than those of the NICB.

b The null hypothesis, tested by Chi-Square, that there are no differences in the groups is rejected with 95 per cent confidence. The differences among and between groups are significant. In the case of the data by longest workweeks, the differences among groups are significant for both the set of data that includes the NICB studies and the set that excludes them.

c The percentage distributions are significantly different when all studies are considered. The difference is not significant for the set of data that excludes the NICB studies.

d The null hypothesis of no difference cannot be rejected with 95 per cent confidence.

e Data are not available for NICB studies.

f Data are available only for NICB studies.

ample, although increasing hours from 48 to 52 is almost certain to result in increased output, about half of the time decreasing hours from 52 to 48 will not result in decreased output. What is true of shortening is not necessarily true of lengthening. In 92 per cent of the 124 cases where the workweek was lengthened, output was increased. Yet, the shortening of hours decreased output in only 48 per cent of the 169 cases studied. Among the many possible explanations of this lack of transposition, the one that seems the most plausible is that, once an output level is achieved, both workers and employers take whatever action is necessary to maintain that level even when workweeks are shortened. Employers work to maintain profits; employees, earnings.

3. The change in work hours is relatively small. When hours were changed more than 15 per cent, in only 16 per cent of the 152 cases was output not less under the shorter workweek. For changes of less than 15 per cent, the comparable figures are 48 per cent of 133 cases. This suggests that small changes in hours, either increases or decreases, have little effect upon output. The increases (decreases) in output per man-hour resulting from a shortening (lengthening) of the workweek are about the same, regardless of how much hours are changed. Thus, although a faster rate of production often compensates for a shorter period of production when there is a small reduction in the workweek, productivity gains are rarely a sufficient offset for large reductions in hours of work. Correspondingly, when hours are increased the increase must be sufficiently large to offset the initial fall in productivity if output is to rise.

4. Workers are on piece rates. In 33 per cent of the cases involving workers on piece rates, as contrasted with 23 per cent of the day worker cases, shorter hours involved no sacrifice of output. By making appropriate adjustments in their rate of output, workers paid according to how much they produce are able to maintain their previous earnings in spite of the change in hours; whereas day workers have no power to alter their earnings and, thus, no incentive to change their output per man-hour.

5. Strenuous jobs are involved. Because workers become fatigued sooner at heavy work than at light, longer hours are more feasible for lighter jobs. Although the over-all percentages of cases when shorter hours resulted in more output, 27 per cent for heavy work and 23 per cent for light work, are not significantly different when all cases are compared, there is a significant difference in the percentages (not shown in Table 1) when only the cases involving 56 hours or more are considered.

Although the conclusions defy quantitative summary, these studies also indicate that shorter hours involve less sacrifice of output when the hours eliminated are relatively inefficient ones (e.g., a half-day on Saturday), the jobs involved are operator paced rather than machine controlled, the work environment concerned is generally unpleasant and fatiguing, the period for which the shorter hours are to be in effect is a relatively long one,[1] the hours reduction occurs in a spirit of cooperation, the workers involved use their additional free time to recuperate rather than to play hard or moonlight, the management involved increases capital investments, and the original capital invested per worker is relatively large. As shown in Table 1, neither the sex of the workers nor the behavior of the wage rate was a differentiating factor.

Hours Reduction Below 40

There is almost no evidence on the hours-output relationship for workweeks less than 40 hours. Among the 1,233 cases cited in Table 1, only seven relate to the shortening of the workweek to less than 40 hours. Since a sufficient number of case studies have not been made, it is necessary to look at more aggregative data. The U.S. Bureau of Labor Statistics publishes data on the average number of hours worked per week for over 200 three-digit and 4-digit manufacturing industries.[2] Information on annual output (represented by value added) is published for many of these same industries by the U.S. Department of Commerce.[3] Between 1949 and 1961, in these industries there were 230 identifiable instances when hours of work either increased or decreased by more than 1.5 hours per week in two consecutive years.[4] For example, in the seamless hosiery industry, the average hours worked in a week changed from 36.9 to 39.0 between 1951 and 1952, from 38.1 in 1957 to 36.4 in 1958, and then back to 38.1 in 1959. These changes represent three of the 230. Since many of the 230 instances concern workweeks under 40 hours, and all instances relate to workweeks under 43 hours, a study of how output behaved when hours were changed provides an indication of what might happen if a general reduction in the workweek were attempted at this time.

Output was generally less when shorter workweeks were scheduled. Shorter hours accompanied less output in all but 5 per cent of the cases.[5] The circumstances under which shorter hours involved greater output and lesser sacrifices in potential output are, unfortunately, not obvious.[6] Regardless of whether the original workweek was as much as 43 hours or as little as 38, hours reduction resulted in about the same loss of output. The change in output was slightly less than proportional to the change in hours when hours were reduced from 43 to 41 just as it was from 38 to 36. Nor does the behavior of the wage rate or the significance of labor cost relative to total cost explain the varied reactions to a change in hours. Industries which granted large wage-rate increases simultaneous with the shortening of the workweek were no more likely to reduce output than industries that held the line on wage rates. And the output of industries in which labor costs represent a relatively more significant portion of total costs reacted no differently than in other industries. Finally, the extent of the change in hours was only slightly better as a predictor of the reaction of output to hours change. Although output tended to increase most with relatively large upward adjustments and to decrease most with relatively large downward adjustments, the differences in magnitude are not conclusive.

On the basis of the meager empirical evidence available, the most that can be said about hours reduction below 40 is that it will almost certainly result in a decrease in total output. If this were not so,

employers inadvertently would be missing an opportunity for increased profits, which is unlikely. The magnitude of the decrease
is not predictable, though it is unrealistic to expect large offsetting
increases in output per man-hour. Although there are instances in
which the shortening of the workweek below 40 hours will cause
output to increase, these instances are exceptions, and the exceptions
do not appear to be predictable. As automation becomes more
advanced, the instances in which workweeks may be reduced to less
than 40 hours without the sacrifice of output may become increasingly common, but at this time fewer hours almost certainly mean less
output.[7]

Arguments Pro and Con

A detailed examination of how changes in the length of the workweek affect output lends credence to the empirical findings cited
earlier. When the workweek is shortened, the effects upon output
are manifold and in both directions: Some effects increase output,
others decrease it. As the workweek becomes shorter and shorter,
there is reason to believe that the balance tends to change from
favoring the output-increasing effects to the output-decreasing ones.

Hours Reduction Tends to Increase Output

With the understanding that each does not apply to all instances
of hours reduction, the reasons why shorter workweeks *increase*
output are listed below.

1. Shorter hours enhance worker efficiency. H. M. Vernon reasons
that each individual has a fixed number of energy units per day
which he offers to his employer; for example, 12 units.[8] While at
work, all 12 energy units are expended. Some of the energy is devoted to output-producing activities; other energy, a constant amount
per hour, is consumed by merely being at work (e.g., sitting, standing), regardless of whether productive activity is in progress. For
example, assume that while at work producing nothing the average
worker uses up one-half unit of energy per hour. If a worker works

10 hours, unproductive activity consumes 5 units and leaves 7 for productive activity. If he works 8 hours, only 4 units are consumed unproductively and 8 are left for production. By shortening the workday, the energy requirement of unproductive activity is reduced and energy units are thereby freed for productive use. As more energy is devoted to production, output increases.[9]

Moreover, by reducing sickness,[10] accidents,[11] and voluntary absenteeism,[12] the shortening of workweeks contributes to increased efficiency and, in turn, greater output. Shorter hours allow men to develop their minds in thinking along creative and inventive lines.

2. Even though labor effort remains constant, output per manhour may be increased as a result of hours reduction. Because the number of hours during which equipment is idle are greater, equipment maintenance may be improved and, in turn, output disrupting breakdowns during regularly scheduled periods of production can be reduced. If shorter hours are accomplished by compressing 6 days work into 5, the relatively inefficient "set up" and "knock down" periods are reduced from 12 to 10. Moreover, worker productivity may increase as a result of the "shock effect." If management is in fact impelled to introduce profit-increasing changes only when existing profit margins are in danger, an hours reduction which increases the per unit cost of production may inspire management to undertake output-increasing, cost-reducing innovations.[13] To the extent that the hours shortening causes the ratio of marginal labor cost to marginal capital cost to rise, the innovations are likely to be capital intensive. The result: more equipment per worker and, probably, higher productivity.

3. Shorter hours bring more people into the labor force by enabling housewives, college students, and older persons, whose activities and/or strength do not allow them to fit a full-time job into their schedules, to enter gainful employment. The effects of reducing the average number of hours worked upon labor supply will be offset, it is argued, by an increase in the number of persons employed.

4. Because more people are employed, income will be distributed

more equally. Shorter hours will give money to those who have the time to spend it and time to those who have the money to spend. The redistribution of income and leisure will increase aggregate demand and, thus, cause an upward pull upon output. If resources are unemployed before the hours reduction, the pull is likely to result in more output, not simply inflationary price increases.

Hours Reduction Tends to Decrease Output

Few persons question the validity of each of the above arguments when original hours are very long, above 60. In some situations, hours reduction does increase efficiency and productivity, reduce absenteeism, increase aggregate labor supply, and stimulate aggregate consumer demand. But, argue a substantial majority of academic economists writing today, most of the output-increasing effects of hours reduction have been achieved already.[14] Further shortening of the workweek will lower the maximum possible GNP.

Already workers have sufficient free time to avoid fatigue and maintain their health. The man-hours gained by the complete elimination of industrial accidents, which are already at a very low level, would provide only a small fraction of the hours lost if the workweek were to be shortened by as little as one hour. Instead of becoming more refreshed during the hours freed by further workweek shortening, workers are apt to spend the additional hours at strenuous play[15] or at another job.[16] Moreover, as workdays are shortened, the relatively inefficient "set up" and "knock down" times become an increasing proportion of total worktime.

H. M. Vernon argues that although more energy is devoted to productive activity as the workday is shortened, the crowding of work hours results in the dissipation of much of this energy. Just as a man increases his oxygen consumption more than proportionally as he walks faster and faster, energy consumption increases with faster work. "To produce a maximum output the worker must shorten his hours of work so as to reduce waste of energy from much standing about, but he must not shorten them so much as to necessitate a very great speed of production with its much more than proportionate call upon his energies."[17] Thus, it is not likely that further reductions in the workweek will stimulate large increases in output per man-hour.

Large increases in labor force participation rates cannot be expected either. Historically, this rate has remained relatively constant in spite of continually shorter workweeks.[18] Expansion in the areas of greatest need, the skilled and professional occupations, can be anticipated least of all. Instead, further shortening of the workweek will reduce supplies of already scarce manpower and create additional bottlenecks.[19]

The heart of the case against further hours reduction relates to its effects upon cost. If weekly pay is maintained under a shorter week, and if the rise in output per man-hour is less than proportional to the decrease in hours, less will be produced for the same labor cost. Labor cost per unit will rise. Depending upon the elasticity of demand for inputs and outputs, prices are likely to be increased and the quantity of product demanded will decrease. Because of this decrease and because capital inputs become cheaper relative to labor, fewer man-hours will be demanded. It is not at all clear whether the purchasing power of labor will be increased; for as prices rise the real incomes of the original workers will decline and as the number of man-hours hired declines the prospects of adding new consumers will diminish. Although the productivity of labor will undoubtedly rise as a result of greater capital expenditures, the cost of production, and probably prices, are also likely to increase. Fewer units of output are likely to be produced at a greater capital cost per unit.[20] The over-all effect upon real incomes is, at best, uncertain.

Additional Considerations

Any conclusions regarding the effect of hours reduction upon output level must be guarded, for so much depends upon the manner in which hours are reduced, the circumstances existing prior to the reduction, and the reactions of employers and consumers. There are arguments on both sides, but the facts show that when isolated firms reduce hours below 40 per week, the output of the firms tends to decrease. What the empirical data of the past cannot tell us is what would happen if a large number of firms were to decrease hours of work simultaneously. What would happen if a new law setting standard hours at, say, 30 were passed? The first-round, single-firm effects of hours reduction can be studied empirically; the secondary and tertiary effects upon the economy as a whole must be considered theoretically.

Theory suggests, for instance, that if hours reduction is effected when there is an unemployed pool of equally efficient workers who are willing to work at the going wage rate, economywide output is likely to increase slightly as a result of the increased spending time of the previous workers and the general redistribution of income. On the other hand, even if workers do not insist upon a wage-rate increase when hours are cut, hours reduction at a time of full employment will force employers to pay overtime premiums, raise marginal resource costs, and almost certainly cause a decrease in output. The decrease in output will be even greater if workers insist upon maintaining previous earnings levels through higher wage rates and if each firm operates as if all other firms are going to cut back production in the face of shorter hours and higher wages.

In short, there are instances in which hours reduction will result in a larger output for the firm and the economy, but it appears that these instances are by now relatively infrequent.

Notes

1. For further discussion see Lionel Robbins, "The Economic Effects of Variations in Hours of Labor," *Economic Journal,* XXXIX (March 1929), p. 27.

2. U.S. Bureau of Labor Statistics, *Employment and Earnings,* Table C-7.

3. U.S. Department of Commerce, *Annual Survey of Manufactures,* Table 1.

4. Because of comparability problems due to the changeover in the Standard Industrial Classification System and the occasional unavailability of data, the changes between some years were not considered.

5. It would at first seem that this is convincing proof that shorter hours

mean less output. But this statistic must be viewed with considerable caution, for the direction of the causal relationship is not clear. The lower output levels in years when workweeks are relatively short may reflect attempts on the part of management to cut back output because of an insufficient demand, and long hours during years of high output may reflect concerted efforts to meet strong demands for products. To the extent that this is true, changes in output levels cause changes in the length of the workweek, not vice versa.

6. To determine these circumstances, four independent variables were regressed first upon percentage change in output per man-hour and then upon a measure closely related to percentage change in total output. The independent variables are (1) the longest number of hours worked (i.e., original hours if the change were a decrease), (2) the ratio of labor cost to total cost, (3) the percentage change in the wage rate, and (4) the percentage change in the length of the workweek. Since none of the simple or partial correlation coefficients was significant, null hypotheses could not be rejected. Neither regression equation passed either the t or the F test. The multiple correlation coefficients were $R = .15$ for total output and $R = .18$ for output per man-hour, both being insignificant.

7. For speculation on how the output-optimum workweek changes overtime, see P. Sargant Florence, *International Labour Review*, XLIII (1941), p. 287, and International Labour Organization, "Repercussions of a Reduction in Hours of Work," *International Labour Review*, LXXIV (1956), p. 30.

8. H. M. Vernon, *Industrial Fatigue and Efficiency*, London, George Routledge and Sons, Ltd., 1921, pp. 47–48.

9. Vernon modifies this statement which would mean, if taken literally, that the greatest possible output would result from the shortest possible workweek. This modification is developed in the next section.

10. Cf. H. M. Vernon, *op. cit.*, pp. 143–149, 161–178; J. Goldmark, *op. cit.*, especially Chap. 5; and NICB, *Research Report No. 4*, pp. 45–46.

11. See U.S. Bureau of Labor Statistics, *Bulletin 917*, p. 37, and *Bulletin 791-A* (Part II), p. 4; H. M. Vernon, *op. cit.*, pp. 182–188 and *Accidents and Their Prevention*, New York, The Macmillan Co., 1936, pp. 67–69; and J. Douglas Brown and Helen Baker, *Optimum Hours of Work in War Production* ("Research Report Series No. 65"), Princeton, N.J., Industrial Relations Section, Princeton University, 1942, pp. 9–10.

12. For examples, see P. Sargant Florence, *Economics of Fatigue and Unrest*, pp. 206–207; U.S. Bureau of Labor Statistics, *Bulletin 917*, pp. 43–45; Brown and Baker, *op. cit.*, p. 9; and NICB, *The Five-Day Week in Manufacturing Industries*, New York, privately published, 1929, pp. 45–46.

13. For further discussion, see Clyde E. Dankert, "Shorter Hours—In Theory and Practice," *Industrial and Labor Relations Review*, XV (April 1962), p. 311, and Herbert R. Northrup and Herbert R. Brinberg, *Economics of the Work Week* ("Studies in Business Economics, No. 24"), New York, National Industrial Conference Board, 1950, p. 39.

14. See statements by Dankert, Lester, Northrup, Reder, *et al.*, in *Hours of Work*, Hearings before the Select Subcommittee on Labor of the Committee on Education and Labor, House of Representatives, 88th Cong., 1st Sess., Washington, Government Printing Office, 1964. This reference will subsequently be referred to as *Hearings*.

15. For further development, see Vincent W. Bladen, "Discussion" of papers on the "Economics of the Shorter Work Week," *Proceedings of the Ninth Annual Meeting of Industrial Relations Research Association* ("Publication No. 18"), Madison, Wisc., Industrial Relations Research Association, 1957, p. 223; and Sebastian de Grazia, *Of Time, Work, and Leisure,* New York, The Twentieth Century Fund, 1962, pp. 63–138.

16. Workers are moonlighting more than ever before. Forrest A. Bogan and Harvey R. Hamel, "Multiple Jobholders in May, 1963," *Monthly Labor Review,* LXXXVII (March 1964), p. 252.

17. H. M. Vernon, *op. cit.,* p. 50.

18. For further discussion, see Edward F. Denison, *The Sources of Economic Growth in the United States and the Alternatives Before Us,* New York, Committee for Economic Development, 1962, p. 58.

19. For more of same, refer to the prepared statement by Melvin Reder, *Hearings, op. cit.,* pp. 725–726.

20. If a plant moves from single to multiple shifts when hours are reduced, it is possible to offset increased labor costs by decreasing capital costs. Of course, such action assumes that the producer is able to market the additional product.

10. Automation, Unemployment, and Shorter Hours

CLYDE E. DANKERT

Department of Economics
Dartmouth College

The most common argument advanced in recent years in support of shorter hours has been the unemployment argument. As a result of the development of automation there has been a widespread feeling, particularly among workers and their leaders, that if we are to provide jobs for all our available workers hours will have to be reduced.

Thus a decade ago, when automation was well under way, one observer declared that "in the last analysis it is this steady increase of leisure that will have to be relied on to solve the problem of the technologically displaced."[1] And the president of the International Longshoremen's and Warehousemen's Union stated in 1958 that "the answer to the machine is shorter hours, with no cut in take-home pay."[2]

The passing of the years has not diminished interest in the policy of shorter hours as a means for coping with the employment impact of technological change. Not only is there still strong support for this policy, but new methods for reducing hours have been suggested —and to some extent applied. To the traditional practice of reducing the length of the workweek there has been added the proposal that the length of the workyear should be reduced, not only by extending the length of the normal vacation period but by the introduction of sabbatical leaves. Moreover, the notion of earlier retirements has come into some prominence.

The unions have been active in pressing for shorter hours, and their efforts have met with some degree of success. While no notable gains have been made recently in reducing the length of the standard workweek—an outstanding exception was the achievement in 1962 of the 25-hour week, with five hours of guaranteed overtime, by Local 3 of the International Brotherhood of Electrical Workers— vacations have been lengthened and more paid holidays have been won. In addition to the efforts made by unions to reduce hours, attempts have been made to alter the hour provisions of the Fair Labor Standards Act.

A Glance at the Past

The unemployment argument for shorter hours is by no means of recent origin. As the following historical references indicate, it was advanced at least as far back as the last century. And interestingly enough, the argument was used under economic conditions that bear a resemblance to those of the last ten years.

In his Annual Report to the AFL in 1887, Samuel Gompers remarked that "the displacement of labor by machinery in the past few years has exceeded that of any like period in our history."[3] Then, after citing various examples of mechanization, he went on to make the frequently quoted observation that "the answer to all opponents to the reduction of the hours of labor could well be given in these words: 'That so long as there is one man who seeks employment and cannot obtain it, the hours of labor are too long.'"

Two years later Gompers expressed a similar view. Referring to "the hundreds of thousands of our fellows, who, through the ever-increasing inventions and improvements . . . , are rendered 'super-fluous,' " he went on to declare that "we must find employment for our wretched Brothers and Sisters by reducing the hours of labor or we will be overwhelmed and destroyed."[4]

Gompers' successor, William Green, some decades later (and when the country was in the midst of the Great Depression) asked a rhetorical question which indicated that his views resembled those of the first AFL president. Speaking at the Federation's 1932 convention, Mr. Green inquired, "Is there any reasonable, sensible-minded man who can believe we could equip industry with machinery and provide [employment] six days per week and eight hours per day . . . for every man and woman willing to work?"[5]

The answer of Mr. Green and of many others at the time was a negative one. In the 1930s, as in the 1950s and early 1960s, there was a common belief that industrial mechanization made shorter hours not only a possibility but a necessity.

Temporary Reductions in Hours

The current advocacy of shorter hours is generally based on two assumptions: first, that the standard work period will be permanently shortened (with the possibility of overtime, however); and second, that take-home pay will not be reduced. But hours could be cut temporarily, and take-home pay instead of being maintained could be lowered. As a matter of fact this is the policy that was commonly discussed, and quite often adopted, in the past. It is also a practice that is in some use today.

Temporarily sharing work, however, does not strike at the root causes of unemployment. All it does is substitute underemployment for unemployment. To some degree this is desirable, but the policy involves a number of dangers. For one thing, if it is pushed too far it may lead not only to sharing work but to sharing misery. This apparently happened to some degree during the Great Depression when the practice of work sharing was widely used.[6] It is not surprising, therefore, to find in union agreements with share-the-work arrangements a provision establishing a floor under hours, thus leading to layoffs if further curtailment is necessary.

Use of the share-the-work policy may also lessen interest in the adoption of measures which will reduce the volume of unemployment rather than just spreading it around. The method of amelioration, in other words, may deflect attention from preventive policies.[7]

It is currently being argued, however, that the policy of shorter hours can itself act in a preventive fashion if instead of having the earnings of the workers (per day or per week) reduced, they are maintained. This is the turn that was given to the shorter-hour argument in the extensive discussions of the issue in the early 1930s, and it is the key aspect of the argument today, as we shall see later.

In 1933 Senator Hugo L. Black and Representative William P. Connery introduced bills in Congress which would have established a 30-hour week in interstate employments, without embodying definite provisions concerning the maintenance of take-home pay. In 1934, however, and after the establishment of the NRA codes which provided for variations in hours, Mr. Connery introduced a bill that would have set up a 30-hour week in all employments and in addition would have required the maintenance of weekly wages.[8]

Much of the discussion of the shorter-hour question now came to be based on the assumption that there would be no reduction in take-home pay. The chief argument in these earlier discussions was the one that occupies a pivotal place in the current discussions of the question, namely, the purchasing-power argument. Clustered around this argument were the themes of industrial mechanization and technological unemployment. Clearly the problem that was debated in the thirties bears a striking similarity to the hours question during the last few years. And many of the specific points advanced on the two sides of the issue in the 1930s are being used today.[9] Indeed, if one wants to examine historical parallels one can go back to the eight-hour campaign of the 1890s and the arguments used then.[10]

Congress did not pass any 30-hour measure in the 1930s, but in

1938, when the country was on the economic upgrade, but still with a considerable amount of unemployment, it adopted the Fair Labor Standards Act. Under this law hours were reduced, first to 44 a week, then to 42, and finally, at the beginning of the third year of the law's operation, to 40. Work, in the covered employments, in excess of these hours had to be compensated at the rate of at least time-and-a-half. Nothing was said in the law about the maintenance of take-home pay.

It was expected that the necessity of paying overtime, as specified in the law, would lead to a certain amount of work sharing, and wage sharing. But, in addition, a considerable number of union agreements in force at the time provided explicitly for work sharing. In a study published in 1940 the Bureau of Labor Statistics revealed that about one-quarter of the workers covered by the 7,000 currently operative collective bargaining agreements it had on file were under work-sharing arrangements.[11]

Fifteen years later the BLS made another study of work-sharing procedures, this time, however, limiting its study to agreements covering 1,000 or more workers. Railroads and airlines were excluded. The Bureau found that only 4 per cent of these agreements contained arrangements for work sharing in lieu of layoffs.[12] There was a heavy concentration of such agreements in the apparel industry, an industry characterized by a high degree of seasonality. The 1940 study did not present statistics on the classes of work sharing found in its investigations, but stated that "many" agreements provided for an equal division of the available work, without layoffs.

In interpreting the figures in Table 1 it should be noted that agreements with layoff provisions may also contain work-sharing (and wage-sharing) arrangements. As a matter of fact, the BLS found that about one-quarter of the 1,347 agreements with layoff provisions provided also for a reduction in hours (in numerous instances to 32 a week) as a means of delaying layoffs. Occasionally, limitations or prohibitions on overtime were specified in the agreements studied, a policy which would also lead to work sharing. It should also be

TABLE 1. LAYOFF AND WORK-SHARING PROVISIONS
IN MAJOR COLLECTIVE BARGAINING AGREEMENTS 1954–1955

	Agreements	Workers (000's)
Number of agreements studied	1,743	7,641.9
With layoff provisions	1,347	5,815.1
With work-sharing provisions	74	524.2
No layoff or work-sharing provisions	322	1,302.6

SOURCE: Bulletin No. 1209, U.S. Department of Labor, Bureau of Labor Statistics, *Ananlysis of Layoff, Recall, and Work-Sharing Procedures in Union Contracts*, p. 2.

observed that work-sharing arrangements (under agreements that provide "exclusively" for them) may have to give way to layoffs, as the BLS points out, if the former policy is no longer feasible.

Work sharing (and wage sharing) as an accompaniment of layoffs is used to a considerable degree in American industry, but as a substitute for the latter policy its use is not extensive. As a matter of fact in recent years the unions have become increasingly interested in restricting management's right to spread work, the chief reason being the liberalization of unemployment insurance benefits and the adoption of supplementary unemployment benefits.[13]

But the central issue before us is not the question of work sharing and wage sharing. It is work sharing and wage maintaining, and it is to this widely debated question that we shall now direct our attention.

The Work-Fund Issue

In much of the popular discussion of the hours question there appears to be a definite conviction that as a result of technological change there is now a permanent shortage of jobs: the "machine" is performing such miracles of production that there are no longer enough employment opportunities to go around. Moreover, the rapid growth in our labor force has served to intensify the problem.

The fixed work-fund idea, and that is what is involved here, is essentially invalid, as economists have long pointed out. Nevertheless, it cannot be disregarded. The present analysis calls for some discussion of the notion.

At the outset it must be granted that in "the short run" there *is* a definite fixity to the amount of work available. The output of industry, and the number of jobs that are open, cannot be greatly increased over short periods. This is a basic reason why a temporary share-the-work policy may be desirable. But the same reason cannot be given for a permanent share-the-work policy, for in "the long run" there is not a fixed work fund. Rather there is what one might call, after the practice of Professor Frank W. Taussig,[14] a work flow.

The size of this flow basically depends on the volume of commodities and services the people want and on the methods used by the economy in satisfying these wants. That the unsatisfied material wants of the American populace are still very large—despite what has been said about the affluence of our society—is readily apparent. In this connection one need mention only our present campaign against poverty.

It is difficult, indeed it is impossible, to reconcile the contention that we have this vast unfulfilled demand for goods with the argument that shorter hours are necessary because of a permanent shortage of work brought about by automation and other technological changes.

Moreover, if it is contended that one of the ways to increase production—in order to satisfy these demands—is to shorten hours, it is impossible to argue that shorter hours are necessary in order to spread the limited amount of work available. In other words, the unemployment argument for shorter hours and the greater production argument are in this respect incompatible.

The conclusion seems clear that, apart from temporary situations, there is no close relationship between the length of the workweek, or workyear, and the volume of unemployment. If such a relationship existed, the volume of unemployment in this country should have greatly decreased over the years. But this has not happened, despite the remarkable reduction that has taken place in the hours of work.

It might be argued that other factors have been operative which have tended to conceal the unemployment decline that has taken place. But this argument is not convincing enough to disprove our main contention.

Testimony on this point is also furnished by a comparison of hours of work and the rate of unemployment (in a given period of time) in a number of different countries. As the figures in Table 2 suggest, short hours and low unemployment do not necessarily go together. Japan, for example, with a 50-hour week in its manufacturing industries, had an unemployment rate in 1960 of only .9 per cent

TABLE 2. HOURS OF WORK AND RATES OF UNEMPLOYMENT
IN SELECTED COUNTRIES

Country	Hours Per Week 1961, Manufacturing	Rate of Unemployment, 1961
United States	39.8	6.7%
France	45.7	.9
Germany (Federal Republic)	45.3	.8
Japan	50.0	.9
United Kingdom	46.8	1.4[a]

SOURCE: *Nation's Manpower Revolution*, Part 3, Hearings Before the Subcommittee on Employment and Manpower of the Committee on Labor and Public Welfare, United States Senate, Eighty-Eighth Congress, First Session, pp. 899, 902, 896. From the statement by R. J. Myers.
[a] Great Britain.

(adjusted to the definition of unemployment in this country) compared with our rate of 6.7 per cent.

The preceding considerations relating to hours of work and unemployment within the United States, and between this country and other countries, suggest that the volume of unemployment in any economy is not a function of the length of its workweek.

The case for shorter hours has been based not only on technological progress but on the rapid growth that is taking place in our population and in the size of our labor force. The latter development, it is felt, makes the specter of job scarcity even more foreboding.

Here again, however, the argument is singularly unconvincing. If the relative amount of unemployment in a country is not closely, and directly, related to the length of its workweek, it is also not related to population and labor force size. Nor is it inevitably tied up with the rates at which the last two magnitudes change. The latter fact is indicated by the figures in Table 3. Again we may point to Japan for a specific illustration of our point. Between 1951 and 1960 the Japanese labor force increased by 25 per cent, compared with an increase of 12 per cent in this country. Yet its unemployment rate was just about one-fifth of ours.

TABLE 3.   CHANGES IN SIZE OF LABOR FORCE, UNEMPLOYMENT RATES, AND GROWTH RATES IN SELECTED COUNTRIES

Country	*Per cent change in Labor Force 1951–1960*	*Unemployment Rate 1960*	*Average Annual Rate of Growth Real GNP, 1951–1960*
Germany (Federal Republic)	18	1.0%	7.2%
Japan	25	1.1	8.7
Sweden	12[a]	1.5[a]	3.7
United States	12	5.6	2.9

SOURCE: Based on *Monthly Labor Review,* September 1962, pp. 970, 972.
   [a] 1961.

The last column in Table 3 is a highly significant one, not only because it furnishes us with the reason why the Japanese unemployment rate was so low, despite its extremely rapid labor force growth—and also despite its relatively long hours of work—but because it points to a key argument of the present chapter, namely, that the best way to attack the job-scarcity problem in this country is not by reducing hours but by increasing our growth rate.

The Purchasing-Power Aspect

The most important aspect of the shorter-hour argument, with its accompanying feature of wage maintenance, is the alleged effect it will have on the volume of purchasing power in the economy. The central idea here is comparatively simple: Reduce the hours of present workers but without impairing their earnings, and turn over the hours of work thus made available to unemployed workers, enabling them to have a regular wage income. The new income of the latter group added to the preserved earnings of the former groups will result in an increased volume of purchasing power. This, in turn, will stimulate the economy to higher levels of growth and to more man-hours of employment.

Such a consummation is, indeed, one devoutly to be wished, but the prospect of attaining these goals is by no means certain. Some serious obstacles are in the way.

To begin with there is the question of cost, particularly the cost of labor. The extent to which wage rates are increased under this policy depends, of course, on the degree to which hours are reduced. Figure 2 in Chapter 1 (see p. 11) clearly illustrates this fact. If, for example, hours were lowered from 40 to 35 per week, with take-home pay remaining the same—and this suggestion has often been made—there would be a wage-rate increase of 14.3 per cent per hour. Presumably the new workers taken on would be paid the higher rates as well as the previously employed workers. Such an increase in cost would have serious consequences.

For one thing it could lead to higher prices which, in turn, could have a number of adverse effects. The increase in money purchasing power accruing to the workers might be largely, if not completely, offset by the drop in the buying power of the dollar. The workers directly involved in the change in hour standards would probably be better off than they were before—since the increase in prices would not be as great as the increase in wages—but other groups would be worse off. Taking the economy as a whole, purchasing power, in real terms, might not be changed at all.[15]

Another possible effect relates to the position of the United States in international trade and to its balance-of-payments problem. In the early 1960s, with competition in the world's markets in a vigorous state and with a serious dollar drain, this aspect of the problem received considerable attention. Fears were expressed that the shorter-hour policy would still further jeopardize our international position. During the last year or two, with the price level rising markedly in a number of the important trading nations, the situation facing this country is not as serious as it was. However, this aspect of the hours problem should not be dismissed.

The extent to which costs would be increased (or be prevented from falling) as a result of shorter hours would vary from industry to industry and from company to company. Various factors, including the relative importance of labor costs and the type of adjustments the individual employer makes to the shorter-hour standards, would be involved.[16] A highly important general factor would be the effect of shorter hours on productivity. This is an issue that was taken up at length in Chapter 9, but a few words should be said on the question at this point.

If hours were to be cut to 35 a week, there is good reason for believing that the reduction in weekly output on the part of the *presently employed* workers would be greater than the increase in output due to the hiring of more workers (assuming new workers were taken on). At the time of the great campaign for the eight-hour day back in the 1890s, Sidney Webb and Harold Cox in supporting the reduction in hours declared that "experience shows that, in the arithmetic of labor . . . two from ten is likely to produce, not eight, but even eleven."[17] Strange things may indeed happen in "the arithmetic of labor," and it is quite possible that at that time there were industries in which more could have been produced in an 8-hour day than in a 10-hour day. Similarly, it is possible that today 5 from 40 may produce not 35 but 41. In other words, it is possible that individual workers, and groups of workers, may produce more in a 35-hour week than in a 40-hour week. It is possible, but not probable.[18] It seems certain that a reduction in hours of such a magnitude would decrease the weekly output of the workers whose hours have been reduced, and that this reduction would more than offset the gain in output consequent upon the hiring of the additional workers.

This would inevitably be the case in those instances where the shorter-hour policy was applied to employments and industries in which the labor market is tight. Here shorter hours would not only result in curtailed production but curtailed employment (at least in terms of man-hours) as well.[19] To guard against this possibility such employments and industries might be exempted from any rigid hours limitation. An arrangement of this general sort, it is interesting to note, was embodied in HR 1680 and HR 9802, two of the hours bills introduced into Congress in 1963–1964. The administrative problems involved in such a flexible hours policy raise grave doubts, however, about its feasibility.

Instead of decreasing hours to 35 a week, a more modest reduction, say to 39 or 38, might be made. Here the adverse production effects would not be as great; in fact, production might be maintained. But the new employment opportunities that might be created would be small in number.

It seems likely that the downward course of hours in the future will be in terms of a continuing series of small jumps, reflected in a shorter workweek, longer vacations, and more paid holidays. This is as it should be. With the productivity of industry increasing we will be able to afford further reductions in hours, and these reductions— if they are not too large—will simply reduce the rate of our industrial growth. They will not make it decline in absolute terms.

Returning again to the purchasing-power argument, it can be said that under conditions of less than full employment it is highly important that effective demand, both for consumers' goods and producers' goods, be increased. In a private enterprise, market economy it is doubtful if this objective can be achieved by exerting pressure on individual employers to decrease hours and maintain take-home pay. If effective demand in the economy as a whole is to be stimulated, it would be best to do it through fiscal and monetary means. We have ample evidence of the expansionary possibilities of these methods; we have little evidence, especially of a current nature, of the expansionary possibilities of the shorter-hour policy.

In general, shorter hours are the *result* of increased productivity and economic growth, not the cause. Leisure is ordinarily a time in which "purchasing power" is used and enjoyed, not a time when it is created. If the way to increase the purchasing power of the nation were to decrease the length of the workweek, we would have found a simple means indeed for coping with some of our most serious economic problems. But this approach is too good to be true.

It should be added that those who argue for shorter hours often state that it is only one policy that should be adopted for dealing with unemployment. But even as *one* policy it is open to the objection we have raised.

Some Further Considerations

In 1962 in discussing a reduction in the standard workweek (from 40 hours) to 35 hours, George Meany spoke of 5 million new jobs being created.[20] This result, apparently, would have come from the transference of 175 million man-hours of work a week from 35 million of the employed workers to 5 million new workers. Our discussion so far points to the conclusion that this estimate is very much too high. But there are still further considerations which support our conclusion, or at least indicate that the creation of any given number of job opportunities does not mean an equivalent decrease of the number of workers unemployed.

1. For one thing there is the factor of occupational mobility. From studies that have been made in recent years, and from ordinary observation, it is clearly evident that many of the unemployed workers are not fitted for the jobs that are, and are becoming, available in our everchanging economy. They do not have the general educational and technical qualifications that these jobs demand.

In a very meaningful sense, unemployment is not a question of maladjustments between the demand for labor and the supply of labor. There is no such thing as a demand for "labor" or a supply of "labor." Instead there are a great many separate demands for specific types of labor, and a great many separate supplies. If, therefore, we speak of the demand for labor, we want to think of it as composed of a vast number of individual demands. As Henry Clay once aptly put it, "The demand for labor as a whole is normally an aggregate of particular demands for discontinuous, dispersed and changing pieces of work."[21] This fact intensifies the seriousness of the unemployment problem for it means that there can be vacant jobs and idle workers coexisting at the same time and in the same place. Thus, if we chopped off 175 million man-hours from the workweek of 35 million presently employed workers, it does not follow that there would be 5 million idle workers who could step into the breach.

2. The separate labor demands and labor supplies not only have educational and skill (and age and sex) characteristics but also location characteristics. Labor, of any type, is wanted at specific places, and it ordinarily has to be "delivered" personally by the one who is selling it.

Now the unfortunate fact is that a considerable number of our idle workers are not able, or inclined, to move from their present locations to expanding labor markets. This characteristic of workers is not new by any means. Almost two centuries ago Adam Smith observed that man is "of all sorts of luggage the most difficult to be transported." This lack of labor "fluidity," if we may borrow an expressive term,[22] adds to the difficulty of the unemployment problem. It also points to the desirability of adopting more far-reaching policies for bringing jobs and workers together. Under any circumstances, geographical immobility is a factor that would lessen the job-creating possibilities of any plan for reducing hours.

3. There has been a certain amount of discussion of the effect shorter hours would have on moonlighting. Some observers have felt that with a 35-hour week a considerable number of workers

would seek a second job; others have argued that the effect of the shorter workweek on moonlighting would be very small.

If workers on a 35-hour week sought a second job it would not be because their earnings have been reduced—we are assuming the maintenance of take-home pay—but because they now have more free time at their disposal. There would seem to be good reason for expecting that under the shorter workweek some workers would either become moonlighters or increase the number of the hours they are already putting in on a second job. The number of such workers should not be exaggerated, however. Not only would many of the workers probably prefer the extra leisure to still higher earnings, but many would have difficulty in finding additional jobs of a suitable nature.

4. The hope for providing additional jobs by establishing a shorter normal workweek might be wholly or partially thwarted by resort to overtime. Instead of taking on new workers, after the standard workweek had been reduced to 35 hours, the employer might prefer to continue working his present employees 40 hours or more, even though hours beyond 35 are now all compensable at the rate of at least time-and-a-half. The great concern that has been evinced during the last few years over this very policy, and the legislative proposals that have been made for coping with the "evil," suggest that the reaction of many employers to the 35-hour week might be different than was expected.[23]

If the punitive rate for overtime were increased from time-and-a-half to double time, the job-spreading effect of reduced hours would be increased. But such a policy would have a variety of adverse consequences, including its unfavorable effect on economic growth. If, however, the policy were forced on employers, by collective bargaining or governmental action, it would be best for it to become applicable not after the 35-hour or 40-hour level but after, say, the 45-hour or 48-hour level. This arrangement would afford the employer considerable freedom of action in meeting exceptional production demands but at the same time would discourage him from working his employees long hours—in some cases weekly hours have been stretched to 60 and beyond.

5. A final factor that would interfere with the job-creating potentialities of shorter hours is of a technical nature. This is the highly fixed relationship that often exists between men and machines. A great deal of capital in the form of machinery comes in large, durable "chunks," and this capital cannot easily be spread over the larger number of workers (after the fashion of the simplified assumption of marginal productivity analysis) that the shorter-hour policy would presumably provide.

Other types of adjustments of a technical or organizational nature might be attempted, but most of these would be of limited effectiveness. Probably the best policy in the type of situation we are dealing with would be to resort to the use of shifts. But this would necessitate a large increase in the volume of business—and of production—and, in already existing plants, could be achieved only gradually. In the meantime the number of new jobs made available would be small.

Conclusions

The use of the shorter-hour policy as a means for coping with the unemployment caused by automation is of very limited usefulness and, if hours are reduced sharply, is economically dangerous. This does not mean, however, that under no circumstances should hours be reduced. In given situations temporary reductions in hours, involving work sharing and wage sharing, may be desirable. And in the economy as a whole some of the future gains in industrial productivity should be "consumed" in the form of increased leisure.

To deal with technological unemployment various policies should be used. One of the greatest needs is to increase our rate of economic growth—an objective that could be easily endangered if hours at present were cut to any large degree. But specific measures for increasing the occupational and geographical mobility of displaced workers are also needed. To advocate one set of policies to the exclusion of the other is economically unwise and socially unjust.

Notes

1. *The Reporter*, April 7, 1955, p. 17.
2. *The New York Times*, September 28, 1958, Sec. 5, p. 16.
3. Samuel Gompers, *Labor and the Employer*, compiled and edited by Hayes Robbins, New York, E. P. Dutton & Co., 1920, pp. 81–83. It is interesting to note that some years earlier another observer stated that "everywhere we meet with the same state of facts. The laborsaving machine is entering every field, and its entrance is to the workman an irresistible command to go." *Atlantic Monthly*, August 1879, p. 137.
4. Quoted in John R. Commons, *et al.*, *History of Labor in the United States*, II, The Macmillan Co., New York, 1918, p. 479.
5. AFL 1932 Convention *Proceedings*, p. 5.
6. *The New Republic*, October 26, 1932, pp. 274–275.
7. For a more detailed discussion of the advantages and disadvantages of spreading work, see Herman Feldman, *Stabilizing Jobs and Wages*, New York, Harper & Brothers, 1940, pp. 118–122.
8. Harold G. Moulton and Maurice Leven, *The Thirty-Hour Week*, Washington, The Brookings Institution, 1935, pp. 4–5.
9. See Moulton and Leven, *op. cit.; The Thirty-Hour Week*, New York, National Industrial Conference Board, 1935, Studies No. 214; "The Thirty-Hour Week: Recovery Standard," in the *American Federationist*, February 1933, pp. 179–186.
10. See, for example, Sidney Webb and Harold Cox, *The Eight Hours Day*, London, Walter Scott, 1891; John Rae, *Eight Hours for Work*, London, Macmillan and Co., 1894; George Gunton, *Wealth and Progress*, New York, D. Appleton and Co., 1894.
11. *Monthly Labor Review*, June 1940, p. 1341.
12. *Monthly Labor Review*, December 1956, p. 1387. Details of the BLS studies are brought together in the Bureau's bulletins no.'s 1189 and 1209.
13. See Sumner H. Slichter, James J. Healy, F. Robert Livernash, *The Impact of Collective Bargaining on Management*, Washington, The Brookings Institution, 1960, pp. 152–153. To promote the policy of work sharing R. Stanton Wettick, Jr., has suggested a plan for modifying our unemployment insurance laws which involves the sharing of unemployment benefits. See his article in the *Labor Law Journal*, November 1964.
14. In his discussion of the wage-fund theory Taussig used the concept of a wage-flow. See his *Wages and Capital*, New York: D. Appleton and Co., 1896, pp. 20–22.
15. For further discussion of this point see Chap. 1.
16. Andrew J. Biemiller of the AFL (who favors shorter hours as a means for dealing with unemployment) takes up these factors in his testimony before the House Select Subcommittee on Labor of the Committee on Education and Labor in *Hours of Work*. See *Hearings*, 88th Cong., 1st Sess., Part 2, pp. 520–521.
17. *Op. cit.*, p. 4.
18. Edward F. Denison has stated that since 1929 reductions in hours have probably resulted in decreases in output. See *The Sources of Economic Growth*

in the United States, New York, Committee for Economic Development, 1962, p. 36.

19. On this point see Professor Reder's statement in *Hearings, op. cit.,* Part 2, p. 724.

20. *AFL–CIO News,* September 8, 1962, p. 1. The same general contention was made back in the midst of the Great Depression by a writer in the *American Federationist* (February 1933), p. 182. Admitting the approximate nature of his calculations, the writer declared that "A 28-hour work week would give work to all."

21. *The Post-War Unemployment Problem,* London, Macmillan and Co., 1929, p. 3.

22. See the chapter on "The Organized Fluidity of Labor," in Sir William Beveridge's *Unemployment: A Problem of Industry (1909 and 1930),* London, Longmans, Green and Co., 1931.

23. The problem of "Fringe Benefits and Overtime as Barriers to Expanding Employment" is discussed by Joseph W. Garbarino in the *Industrial and Labor Relations Review,* April 1964. See also Professor Northrup's discussion in Chap. 1.

11. Hours of Work and the General Welfare*

MELVIN W. REDER

Department of Economics
Stanford University

To prevent this chapter from becoming a methodological exercise in the application of welfare criteria, I shall posit some criteria that I hope will be widely acceptable and proceed without entering into a lengthy defense of them.

1. Welfare will be said to increase if (a) two parties, an employer and an employee, voluntarily agree to terms of employment and no third party is injured thereby; or (b) if claims of injury to third parties can either be rejected or acceptable compensation provided for those injured.

2. Where third parties are injured, there is no unanimity on how to appraise the gains and losses of the individuals involved—and/or how to determine what constitutes acceptable compensation for those injured. Each case will be considered separately, and where I believe wide—though probably never universal—agreement exists, I

* This chapter was begun while I held a Ford Faculty Fellowship in 1961–1962.

will indicate what is believed to be the consensual view of the equities of the matter. The consensus to which reference is made is a consensus of professional economists; that is, "consensus" means my opinion of what a "preponderant majority" of economists think about a certain issue. Obviously, a consensus does not always exist.

In restricting reference to economists, there is no intent to deprecate the opinions of others. It is simply that economists have thought about and discussed the issues of this chapter more explicitly than others, and that I can better guess at their views.

3. Though we do not believe the rule to be universally applicable, many of the judgments made under the second criterion can be rationalized as follows: Where a voluntary agreement among private parties is reached and/or a government action is undertaken, the presumption is that the gains of the parties involved or of those to be directly benefited (by the government) are appreciably larger and therefore more important than the losses of those incidentally injured. This might be termed the "presumption of the negligibility of indirect effects."

But particular considerations may tell against the presumption, and even defeat it. ("Defeating the presumption" implies that the government ought to prevent the action, or its recurrence, or compensate those injured by it.) One such consideration is that substantial losses of income or capital may befall particular individuals as a result of the action. The weight of this consideration is enhanced if the injured parties are less affluent than the typical member of the community. Another consideration is that the action involves use of "improper means," e.g., it involves creation and/or utilization of monopoly controls over a wage rate or price. Yet a third consideration might be that the action (allegedly) injures public health, safety, or morals. Other considerations might be mentioned, but there is little point in doing so; they will be discussed where they apply. Despite the importance of these various "considerations," it will be seen that the presumption is not empty.

Now let us set forth a few assumptions upon which the argument will be based:

1. Under peacetime conditions, the lifetime pattern of working hours for each person is such that (as of the mid-1960s) there are no appreciable gains in health, safety, or length of life that could be made by further alterations; that is, all such gains as could be made by reducing the workweek, ending child labor, etc., already have been made. While it is possible that a few marginal exceptions to this statement might be found, I do not believe that there will be serious objection to the statement that in the mid-1960s, considerations of health and safety are not an important factor in public policy decisions concerning hours of work.*

2. In accordance with our welfare criteria, there is a presumption that the levels of effective demand for labor and of money-wage rates should be adjusted to one another so that every person is able to work as much as he chooses at the going rate.† Economists will disagree as to whether this adjustment can be better achieved by the monetary-fiscal authority responding to exogenous movements in money wages or, *à la* Friedman, Shaw, *et al.*, by prescribing permissible variations in the money supply narrowly, and compelling money-wage rates to adjust thereto. Few would deny, however, that either type of adjustment was preferable to rationing employment (see below) and restricting the level of per capita output to levels below those attainable.

However, outside the ranks of professional economists there are those (e.g., representatives of organized labor) who might prefer to reduce per capita output and ration jobs rather than accept money

---

* Of course, this statement presupposes a given state of medical knowledge. Obviously, new discoveries about the aging process, for instance, could upset this assumption.

† This is, of course, too simple. Different types of workers have different wage rates which must be adjusted to one another as well as to the level of effective demand. However, it will serve to indicate that it is assumed that it is better to reduce general unemployment by increasing demand for labor than by rationing employment opportunities.

wage cuts or forego some minimally acceptable rate of money-wage increase. Such a preference might reflect either high relative valuation of money-wage increases or disbelief that their sacrifice would improve the terms of trade-off between inflation and underemployment or—most likely—both. But whatever the reason for this preference, it is sufficiently deep and widespread to require acceptance as a datum for monetary-fiscal policy, at least in the short run. Therefore, I assume that money-wage rates are a datum for monetary-fiscal policy, and that in the event the current *level* of effective demand is judged inadequate to provide sufficient employment opportunities, the preferred action is to increase the level of demand rather than to curtail labor supply and/or ration available work opportunities. However, reducing the workweek will be considered as a second or higher order best, in the event that the preferred action cannot be taken.*

3. It is assumed that there is no attempt to use working hours as an implement to manipulate labor's share of the national income. Before World War I, labor spokesmen often talked as though they thought that by reducing the working day to eight hours, they could force up the real-wage rate and (presumably) increase labor's share.† However, in recent years there has been no one who has seriously proposed a policy to implement this view—at the national level (particular sectors are discussed below)—and even if someone had, its chance of success would be highly dubious. Not the least of the difficulties involved concerns the character of the aggregate production function; if its elasticity of substitution (between labor and capital) is greater than unity, labor's share must fall as the number

*This, of course, does not preclude the possibility that in particular sectors of the economy reducing weekly hours may be an appropriate short-run response to a decline in *relative* demand.

† It is attributing too much to (most) eight-hour day pamphleteers to suggest they thought in terms of labor's share. For the most part, they were innocent of any notion of demand elasticity, but talked as though they assumed it was less than unity (for labor), i.e., "reducing the hours increases the pay."

of man-hours employed declines relative to the quantity of capital.*

4. It is assumed that in the United States, at present, there is a consensus that children should not seek gainful employment before the ages of 16–18, except possibly during vacations and holidays.

5. It is implicit in my second assumption that there is no societal preference for more work (and output) and less leisure, or the reverse, than individuals willingly agree to at existing real-wage rates. However, since some readers may be surprised at my failure to consider national goals of any sort, I shall make explicit the individualist bias embedded in Assumption 2.

This assumption differs from that made by E. F. Denison in his analysis of growth prospects for the American economy.[1] Denison says that "unless employers and employees know that amount by which production is impaired by shorter hours, rational decisions are impossible. I do not believe either employers or employees have this information. Nor, with the present great uniformity of standard hours, can it be supposed that competition among firms, leading to expansion of those arriving at the correct level of hours and contraction of those that do not, serves as a substitute mechanism to assure arrival at a correct level."[2] My argument is independent of any such factual judgment as this; indeed, the correctness of this judgment is debatable.

Apart from the effect of legislation (and/or union policy) designed to limit weekly hours, it is by no means obvious that the competitive process does any worse in providing a variety of patterns of annual and lifetime hours than in generating a spectrum of qualities and types of product. Even though the length of the workweek is fairly well standardized, there is a great variety of arrange-

---

* The form of the aggregate production function most commonly used, the Cobb-Douglas, implies that the elasticity of substitution between labor and capital is unity, and that labor's share is independent of the quantity of either factor. The question of whether aggregate production functions are "valid" and, if so, what their characteristics are is presently one of the liveliest areas of current controversy in the field of economics.

ments for paid holidays, vacations, sick leaves, retirement ages, over-time work, opportunities for moonlighting, etc., so that workers have a variety of options concerning annual and lifetime hours. Whether the variety is sufficient is a good question, but similar questions may be asked concerning shoe sizes, dress styles, housing accommodations, etc. The answers to such questions are not obvious, but *are* matters of fact.

It may be, as Denison's remarks suggest, that the external econ-omies of having the same working hours as "most" other firms are such that innovations (deviations from the common pattern of weekly hours) by any one firm would reduce its profits,* even though everyone would benefit if all firms together adopted a new set of conventions concerning weekly hours. If so, the impetus for change might have to come from government, and substantial research would be required in order to decide what pattern of working hours was "socially optimal." However, the research necessary to ascertain this pattern has not been done and until it is it will be difficult to appraise the validity of Denison's conjecture. The argument of this chapter assumes that potential gains from government intervention of this kind are negligible; however, Denison's contrary opinion should be borne in mind.

Restrictions on Working Hours

Concern about working hours has, in recent years, come to be recognized as a problem in the allocation of time between work and leisure over a lifetime rather than during a day or a week. This recog-nition is not confined to academic investigators but has spread to government officials and union leaders who now demand sabbatical years, early retirement, etc., in addition to (or in lieu of) shorter workweeks. However, in this section it will simplify discussion if we

---

* That is, the gains from being able to send and/or receive orders and other communications from customers and suppliers, and the desire of workers to have leisure at "regular" times, might make deviations from the norm (pri-vately) antiproductive, and raise the supply price of labor into the bargain.

concentrate upon number of hours per lifetime and leave questions of their intertemporal allocation until later.

Despite ruminations, profound and otherwise, on whether man has enough leisure or wisely uses what he has, there is little political concern about the problem *except* in the context of a supposed shortage of employment opportunities. Whatever family sociologists conclude about the effects of moonlighting on family life, men of affairs will not be impelled to action unless they believe that one man's second job is another's unemployment. Similarly, the pressure behind the drive to impede overtime work and shorten the standard workweek is the desire to reduce unemployment, and/or prevent it from arising, through a more equal sharing of opportunities to work.

I am concerned primarily with the question of whether legislation and/or union pressure to compel some individuals to relinquish employment they are able to obtain—so that it may be available for others—promotes the "general welfare." To analyze this matter it is convenient to posit a double dichotomy: long-run—short-run and over-all unemployment-sectoral unemployment. This yields us four classes of which one, long-run-sectoral, is assumed to be empty. Let us now consider the others.

Long-run Over-all Unemployment

Like most economists, I find it extremely difficult to justify employment rationing in a long-run context. As Assumption 2 implies, if there is an *over-all* shortage of employment opportunities, effective demand should be increased. Where economists differ from those who fear starvation from cybernation is in their confidence that if the level of money demand is expanded sufficiently, the marginal productivity of labor can be brought into equality with its marginal disutility for all individuals who do any work, and at a positive real-wage rate. Those who disagree on this point will hardly be converted by anything that can be said here, while others need no convincing. Therefore it will be assumed that in the long run we can, by expanding the public sector if in no other way, provide as many hours of work (at a positive real-wage rate) as the population chooses to perform.

This does not say very much. For example, it could be that the effect of technical progress is to reduce the "free market" real-wage rate (in terms of consumers' goods) well below its present level so that the only way to avoid an unpalatable shrinkage in labor's share of the national income would be artificially to stimulate labor intensive outputs through expansion of the public sector or in some way to restrict labor supply.* It is, indeed, conceivable that had it not been for the secular expansion of the public sector and the semicompulsory reduction in the workweek during the past half-century this would already have occurred in the United States. To refute this charge—often made in varying guises by critics of capitalism—is no easier than to support it. But if the charge is true, it provides good evidence for the existence of a strong socio-political mechanism that works as a counterbalance to technical progress in limiting unemployment.

Historical speculation aside, I am confident of the acceptability of Assumption 2 for the range of choices (between expanding public-sector employment and rationing employment opportunities) that society has confronted hitherto. However, if to avoid "intolerable" unemployment, we were compelled drastically to expand the public sector† and (via taxation) substantially to substitute public for private consumption, the resulting twist to relative marginal valuations *might* lead many people to prefer employment rationing and a lower tax bill. This raises interesting problems of a purely theoretical nature, but their pursuit would take us rather far from our main theme.

In short, for the long run, the threat of *over-all* unemployment should be handled by increasing effective demand, as long as doing so does not alter the relative sizes of the public and private sectors "too much." If this condition is not satisfied, Assumption 2 may not hold. However, this reservation is probably not very important

---

* This might be interpreted as a sophisticated version of the argument for long-run technological unemployment, the naïve version of which was rejected in the preceding paragraph.

† It is far from obvious that this has ever been true, or ever will be.

for purposes of public policy decision in the foreseeable future, where proposed changes in the relative sizes of the public and private sectors are small.

Short-run Sectoral Unemployment

A convenient case to analyze is that which arises when technical progress operates to lower unit costs in one sector or industry relative to another. Output and employment expand in the Reduced-Cost sector and decline in the other. During the adjustment process, which is sometimes quite lengthy, there may arise a considerable demand for overtime work in the Reduced-Cost (RC) sector, while workers are simultaneously unemployed in the Shrinking (S) sector. Restricting overtime work in RC will both raise marginal cost and curb output in this sector, with the result that some orders and employment will be transferred to S. The workers in RC who are harmed would be earning supernormal quasi-rents in the absence of restriction on overtime, while those in S would be partially unemployed. Therefore, if weekly earnings were higher in RC than in S,* the widespread (though not universal) agreement that greater equality of earnings is (*ceteris paribus*) desirable, implies that overtime work should be curbed.

However, the effect on efficiency clearly would be adverse. Output would be diverted from low to higher cost firms. Also the reallocation of additional workers to RC from S and other parts of the economy would be impeded by curbing the difference in weekly earnings between RC and S. But to weigh equality against efficiency in such cases is not easy and a government or union engaged in restricting overtime could argue that considerations of distributive justice outweigh those of efficiency.

How one balances considerations of efficiency against those of equality depends not only upon his values, but also upon his judgment as to the magnitudes involved. If the loss of real output is

---

* Be it noted, that this is a big "if" the satisfaction of which is far from universal.

judged to be small, and the per capita income of the *RC* workers much greater than that of the workers in *S,* some economists probably would join their egalitarian friends in other fields in endorsing such measures as restricting overtime work. But the greater the hypothesized output loss, and the smaller the income difference between the two groups, the less prone will economists and others be to sacrifice efficiency to distributive justice. In judgments of this character interpersonal differences among the judges in "marginal rates of substitution between efficiency and justice" are compounded by the practical difficulty of making the implied measurements.

However, substantial agreement can be obtained on the proposition that restricting the hours of more efficient workers is a poor way to raise the incomes of the less efficient. Some form of social insurance would be clearly superior. Consider: The risk of facing a decline in the demand for one's labor services through technical progress, change in tastes, etc., is something shared by most wage earners. Suppose there were an arrangement by which, in exchange for premiums paid from wages, those whose earnings declined below some previously attained level would be paid a supplement that would bring them up to (or near) their previous level. Such an arrangement could satisfy the egalitarian sentiments that lead to condoning counterproductive activities, without requiring us to forego the real output that such activities impose.*

The spirit of such a proposal is the same as that of unemployment insurance and severance pay. It is not my intent to consider the details of such a proposal beyond indicating that it is by no means a new institutional departure and could be grafted onto our present system of unemployment insurance. Indeed, what the proposal would amount to is a combination of relating unemployment benefits to past income; a (probable) increase in the level of benefits; an exten-

---

* That is, we could get agreement that curbs on working hours should be discouraged (see below) if we could provide income protection for those who could be unemployed in the absence of such curbs.

sion of benefits to cover partial as well as total unemployment; and, finally, an integration of unemployment insurance with provision for severance pay and retraining of displaced workers.*

The rationale of proposing such an extension of social insurance is that in a changing economy particular groups of workers suffer from unemployment, but the incidence of such unemployment is difficult to predict in advance. Because most workers are inadequately insured against the economic effects of this contingency, when it befalls them they attempt, through collective bargaining and political pressure, both to increase their employment opportunities and to control the distribution of whatever opportunities are available.

The devices used frequently reduce man-hour productivity as well as ration hours of work, and are widely condemned as featherbedding. (Make-work rules, whether imposed by unions or legislation, have the same motivation and the same counterproductive effects as curbs on working hours, and for the next few paragraphs I treat them as one phenomenon.) Yet there is considerable sympathy for the workers who require these restrictive practices in order to obtain "reasonably steady" employment.† It is because of this sympathy that it has been impossible to mobilize public support for a campaign to proscribe "make-work" union rules. However, if a loss of employment opportunities could be accepted as a normal incident of economic life and were adequately insured against, a different attitude might be adopted toward counterproductive practices that are presently accepted, *faute de mieux,* as a substitute for job insurance. Given such insurance a worker whose job became a casualty of economic change would, depending upon his age, receive retraining benefits or be permitted to retire earlier than otherwise. *If these benefits were adequate,* many economists presently unwilling to

* This last suggestion is nonessential, though desirable.

† This sympathy is usually conditional upon the "blamelessness" of the workers involved. If, for example, they are believed to demand excessive wage rates (e.g., plumbers), they will not get much sympathy.

sacrifice distributional considerations to greater efficiency would become willing to do so and might well create a consensus against curbs on weekly hours and/or the use of less than the most efficient techniques of production.

To achieve such a consensus among economists, it would be essential that the insurance benefits be adequate, and participation universal (i.e., compulsory). Benefits will be "adequate" when they are high enough to assuage the social conscience of the "welfare judges" in the face of unemployment, and permit the formation of a consensus in favor of, *inter alia,* freedom of contract in determining working hours. It is necessary that the insurance scheme be compulsory because the individuals to be considered include third parties whose social conscience must be satisfied. If, when confronted with an individual who chose to bear the risk to save the premium, the community would let him take the consequences of adversity, compulsion would be unjustified. It is clear, however, that in most advanced communities this is not the case, and that therefore some individuals may be compelled to join the scheme (and pay), irrespective of whether they consider it in their own interest to do so.*

The practical implication of these remarks is that the work inhibiting provisions of the Fair Labor Standards Act (FLSA), Old Age Insurance law, and various state laws could be advantageously traded (repealed) for a suitable extension of social insurance to give further (and substantially greater) protection against economic loss from unemployment. By "advantageously traded," I mean that a consensus of economists would approve such a trade. It is doubtful that a consensus could be found for repealing these laws in the absence of the proposed trade. (The question of union rules on overtime is considered below.)

---

* That is, where a community will not let a person starve "no matter what," his implied minimum food intake becomes a public good whose rational use may require that he be compelled to purchase this food (or a claim thereto) before using his income for any other purpose. Obviously, the community's social conscience implies restraints on individual liberty. Compulsory membership in the social security system illustrates this point.

Short-run Over-all Unemployment

In this context, the main effect of requiring penalty rates for over-time—or forbidding it outright—is to worsen the trade-off between unemployment and inflation for purposes of monetary-fiscal policy. This effect arises because workers are not completely interchangeable. If they were, then it would be possible to divide the weekly hours of work to be performed throughout the nation by the number of job applicants and give all an equal number of hours of work without any adverse effect on productive efficiency or levels of cost.

Manifestly, this is not the case. As an economy moves closer to a level of full employment, the demand for particular workers (distinguished by occupation and location) tends increasingly to exceed the supply available at the standard workweek, while others are still underemployed. While the supply of overtime labor at straight-time rates is not known, it is generally believed that much of that currently hired would be available at less than the mandatory "time and a half." If so, the marginal costs of some firms would be lower, at any given level of GNP, in the absence of FLSA than at present. Since there is no reason to suppose that the marginal costs of any firms would be raised (by abolishing FLSA), I shall assume that at a given level of straight-time money wages, an economywide index of marginal costs is higher in the presence of FLSA than it would be in its absence.

To put the matter more systematically, consider Figure 1 on p. 193, on whose horizontal axis we measure real GNP as a percentage of "capacity GNP" and on whose vertical axis we indicate the price level (reciprocal of the GNP deflator). Capacity GNP is the maximum GNP obtainable with a given productive technique, capital stock, population, and tastes for leisure; capacity GNP is termed "full-employment GNP" and the "degree of employment" attained is assumed to increase with real GNP (measured as in Figure 1).

The curves S and S' are short-run aggregate supply curves drawn on the assumption of given technique, capital stock, level of straight-time money-wage rates, and an average "mark-up coefficient." S refers to an economy with present legal requirements and union practices concerning overtime pay and S' to an economy identical in every way with that to which S refers except that all legal requirements for overtime premiums are repealed and union policy permits at least somewhat lower overtime rates than now prevail. The ordinate of each point on these curves is the supply price—the price level—at which that rate of GNP would be produced under the specified conditions. The mark-up coefficient is a catchall for the various factors (e.g., taxes, interest, monopoly power) that affect the relation between the level of straight-time money-wage rates and the price level (i.e., the straight-time real-wage rate). For our purpose the most important thing about the mark-up coefficient is that it is assumed to be constant.

At low levels of GNP, S and S' are assumed to be identical, as overtime work will be unimportant. At higher levels of output and employment S rises above S' and is more steeply inclined at every abscissa. The higher levels of S mean that the straight-time *real*-wage rate must be lower at any level of GNP (greater than V) under S than under S'; i.e., given the straight-time money-wage rate, W, the price-level will be higher under S than under S'. The steeper slope of S means that to move from any given level of GNP to a higher level, a greater increase in the price level (and in the level of marginal cost) must be accepted with S than with S'.*

To see the implications of this model for monetary-fiscal policy, suppose that Figure 1 holds at a given instant and that through time both S and S' are subject to opposing pressures from increasing man-hour productivity which tends to reduce their ordinates (at all abscissae) at some given annual rate, and from secular increases in W which tend to elevate these ordinates at a given annual rate. For

---

* The justification for assuming that S is more steeply inclined that S' is that the closer the economy gets to full employment the larger is the fraction of the required increase in man-hours worked (on account of an increment in GNP) that must be paid overtime rates.

simplicity, suppose that the net effect of collective bargaining is to make W rise at the same percentage rate as man-hour productivity so that the shapes and positions of S and S' will remain unchanged through time so long as the relevant abscissa in Figure 1 is unchanged.*

FIGURE 1

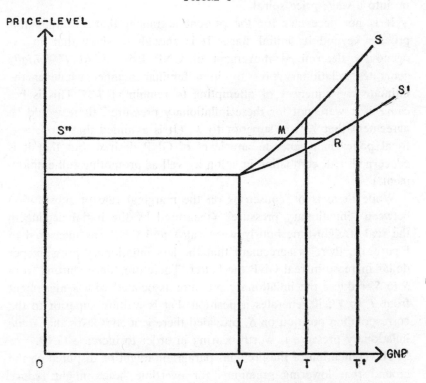

* The assumption that W (the straight-time money-wage rate) varies proportionately with man-hour productivity is arbitrary though not unrealistic. Assuming that W grew at some multiple of man-hour productivity other than unity would not alter the argument, but making W depend upon the level of GNP would. I doubt that the resulting complications would be of great practical importance and, in any case, they cannot be considered for reasons of space.

To assume that S and S' would be unchanged when W grows at the same rate as man-hour productivity implies that in each "year" the economy is a

However, an increase in GNP from T to T' would lead to a fall in W relative both to man-hour productivity and the price-level. Our assumption concerning the relation between W and man-hour productivity implies that this would lead to a more rapid rate of increase in W, as straight-time money wages sought (vainly) to catch up with prices. This, in turn, would lead to a upward shift of S and S' and so on into a wage-price spiral.

It is not necessary for the present argument that we study this process beyond its initial stage. It is enough to show that an exogenously determined movement of GNP from T to T' *initially* generates inflationary pressure in a familiar manner whatever the ultimate consequences of attempting to remain at T'.* This is because if it were not for these inflationary pressures, there would be agreement that T' was superior to T. (It is assumed that monetary-fiscal policy can generate any level of GNP desired, but that it is concerned with combating inflation as well as promoting full employment.)

While there is no consensus on the marginal rate of substitution between "inflationary pressure" (measured by the initial decline in the real straight-time hourly wage rate) and GNP (as measured in Figure 1), there is agreement that the less inflationary pressure per dollar increase in real GNP the better. Therefore, since shifting from S to S' reduces the inflationary pressure associated with a movement from T to T', it generates a position that is welfare superior to the corresponding position on S, provided there is a consensus that *some* inflationary pressure is worth bearing in order to increase GNP.

The contention of the previous paragraph might be disputed on the ground that lowering premiums for overtime hours might reduce

---

scalar multiple of what it was one year earlier, with the scale factor being the growth rate in man-hour productivity which is assumed equal to the growth rate in the real-wage rate.

* To speak of initial effects suggests lagged reactions. Therefore assume that W responds to changes in the price-level (e.g., via escalator clauses) with a lag so that Figure 1 will consistently represent a movement from T to T' for a short interval.

labor's share of the national income, a consequence that many economists would consider undesirable. But whether this actually happened would depend upon the manner in which reductions in premiums for overtime work were made. It is always possible, in principle, to offset a given reduction in labor's share that results from a decline in overtime pay by appropriately increasing straight-time rates.

What this would mean, in terms of Figure 1, is that instead of moving from S to S', the economy would move to S'' which lies above S' for a range from O to R and then becomes identical with it.* To the left of M, S'' lies above S (as well as S') because the straight-time wage rates are higher (by hypothesis), which outweighs the effect of the lower overtime premiums because at low levels of GNP overtime hours are a relatively small part of the extra employment resulting from incremental increases in GNP. At M, the effect of higher straight-time rates is balanced by lower overtime premiums, and to the right of M is more than balanced so that S'' lies below S to the right of M.

Accomplishing a shift from S to either S' or S'' would not be easy, but neither would it be impossible. Obviously, legal requirements for overtime pay would have to be repealed, and beyond this there is the question of union policy. Most economists (including myself) would oppose granting government agencies power to order unions to change their rules or collective bargaining demands concerning overtime pay or other economic matters. However, when a consensus forms on a particular issue (e.g., discrimination against Negroes in union admission), moral suasion becomes an extremely potent instrument of government policy.† Once the commitment to maintain

---

* If the schedule of overtime rates was the same under S' and S'', the diagram would imply that all man-hours employed to the right of R were paid overtime rates. To avoid this, imagine that in moving from S' to S'', the schedule of overtime premiums is lowered in such a way as to produce the state of affairs depicted.

† Of course, the consensus needed for this purpose is far wider than a consensus of economists.

"full enough" employment is sufficiently firm and accepted as such, it may be possible to induce unions to abandon penalties for overtime work—they may even do it of their own accord. Of course, it would be far easier to persuade unions to do this once they were free to swap some or all of the present overtime premiums for higher straight-time rates. This would now be impossible, with rare exceptions, under FLSA.

Trade Union Policy and Individual Choice

One of the complaints most frequently made against regulation of working hours, either by labor organizations or government, is that it prevents individuals who have unusual tastes in working hours from gratifying them. By the same token it penalizes labor users with atypical (time) patterns of demand. As a result, regulations aimed at standardization of working hours systematically violate our first welfare criterion. However, rationalization for such violations can be framed in terms of our second criterion. For example, it can be (and is) argued that preventing some individuals from working on Sundays gives an opportunity for a sabbath holiday to many others who desire it, but whose "bargaining power" is inadequate to obtain it. Whatever one's opinion of this argument, it is not clear that there is a consensus against it. Consequently I shall not condemn collective regulation of work-leisure patterns per se. Instead I will try to indicate how, in some important cases, the objectives of "hours regulation" can be achieved without sacrificing so much of the benefits of individual choice of working hours as is entailed by legislative or union rules applicable to everyone alike.

Because there is not space for analyzing all the various institutional impediments to the free choice of a workweek, I shall consider only one of the most important: the requirement (of FLSA and various state laws) that premium rates be paid for weekly hours in excess of 40. Clearly, this legal requirement is a restriction on free collective bargaining that impedes mutually advantageous trades of higher straight-time rates for overtime premiums of less than "time and a half" as required by law.* Yet many union spokesmen support the present requirements of FLSA and go further to urge that premium rates for overtime begin at 35 instead of 40 weekly hours and even be raised to twice the straight-time rate.[3]

But if this is what they want, why don't they demand it through collective bargaining, as a few unions already have? One reason, to be sure, is that what is legally required need not be bargained for, so that legislation would enable unions to conserve their bargaining power for other ends. But more important is the conflict of interest among union members on this issue. Most unions discriminate, both in layoff and distribution of overtime, in favor of workers with greater seniority. These workers have much greater assurance of steady work than their juniors and consequently are unwilling to sacrifice potential gains in weekly earnings to obtain shorter hours and a redistribution of employment opportunities in favor of junior workers. Rather than provoke intraorganizational conflict, union leaders prefer to have the issue settled by legislative fiat for which they need accept no responsibility.†

This type of conflict over the distribution of jobs suggests that there are unexploited opportunities to increase welfare by mutually advantageous exchanges of employment opportunities for junior workers against higher hourly compensation and less work for seniors. Outright sales of employment opportunities are rare and there would be serious resistance to any attempt overtly to spread the practice.

---

* Put in a slightly different way, this says that the requirement of premium pay for overtime work (whether imposed by union policy or law) of g times the straight-time rate, either makes the straight-time rate obtainable (through bargaining) lower or strikes longer, or both, than if the required premium rate were h. ($g > h \geqq 1$.) This point is argued in more detail in M. W. Reder, "The Cost of a Shorter Work Week," *Proceedings of the Ninth Annual Meeting of the Industrial Relations Research Association*, pp. 207–221, especially pp. 210–215.

† This implies that union spokesmen feel free to advocate legislation whose effects are such that they would not dare demand it at the bargaining table for fear of membership wrath.

Fortunately, there is more than one way to skin a cat, and a number of unions have begun implicitly to build exchanges of the above kind into their contracts.

In essence, increasing pensions relative to hourly wages combined with earlier retirement, sabbatical years for workers with long seniority, etc., are methods of shifting the components of the collective bargaining package currently "purchased" so as to favor senior workers. But these fringes usually involve a relative decline in the annual working hours of senior workers (without decrease of annual earnings) and a corresponding increase in employment opportunities available to junior workers. Thus, by sacrificing current wage gains otherwise attainable in favor of paid leisure that is distributed disproportionately to senior workers (by relating size of benefit to length of service), collective bargaining is performing a de facto exchange of foregone wage increases by all workers for paid leisure that disproportionately benefits older ones. As one facet of this trade younger workers get increased hours of work as replacements for their seniors.*

Some of the costs of this method of providing paid leisure could be reduced by permitting the employer some freedom to decide the time when extended vacations, etc., are to commence. Moreover, it would also be advantageous to the employer to be able to recall vacationing workers as needed to handle peak loads, etc. Conversely, it would be disadvantageous to the employees. This suggests that it might be possible for unions to trade flexibility of work schedules for older employees in exchange for more liberal benefits. Indeed, a union could go further and give high seniority employees a choice among various options ranging from wide freedom to schedule one's leisure to being continuously at management's disposal on short notice; the less attractive options would, of course, be associated with greater compensation. These various possibilities are not academic fancies,

---

* Of course, this still implies union regulation of hours, and leaves us some distance from individual bargaining. However, it is likely to represent a substantial improvement over employment rationing by curbing overtime work.

but are rather modest extensions of current trends in collective bargaining practice. Where applicable, they are very much to be preferred to crude over-all job rationing via penalty rates for overtime.

Notes

1. E. F. Denison, *The Sources of Economic Growth in the United States and the Alternatives Before Us,* New York, Committee for Economic Development, 1962, pp. 36–40.

2. *Ibid.,* p. 38.

3. See the testimony of various union spokesmen in *Hours of Work,* Hearings before the Select Subcommittee on Labor of the Committee on Education and Labor, House of Representatives, 88th Cong., 1st Sess., 1964, Part 2, especially that of A. J. Biemiller and N. Goldfinger, pp. 511–552.

Index